SJ   8 35

Fn Esther

Best wishes

The Romance
of
Michigan's Past

Allan Pinkerton, America's original private eye, dashes down the tracks near Adrian to prevent a train wreck in 1854.

THE ROMANCE OF
MICHIGAN'S PAST
by
Larry B. Massie

The Priscilla Press
Allegan Forest, Michigan
1991

Cover by Judi Miller Morris
Title graphic by Devon Blackwood
Printing by Bookcrafters, Chelsea, MI

ISBN   0-9626408-1-6
First Edition - August 1991

For Adam, Wallace and Larry II, my boys

TABLE OF CONTENTS

Preface

This is a book for those who get a lump in their throat when they see a highway sign proclaiming: "Welcome to Michigan." It's for those who feel an emotional attraction to these two great peninsulas, the big lakes that lap their shores, the musical, magical place-names that dot the map and, especially, the fascinating men and women who have rendered Michigan a place like no other.

This is not a book about famous politicians, generals and wealthy industrialists. You can read about them in the textbooks. Instead, let me to introduce you to a cast of colorful characters who never made it into the traditional history books. They all have two things in common - their destinies became intertwined with that of the Wolverine State - and their exploits make mighty interesting reading.

Most marched to the sound of a different drummer- some were saints, others rogues - all were eccentrics. Some talked to ghosts, others walked around naked as the day they were born. Some lived in communes - in the 1840s - others rode the wilderness trails on horseback, preaching the gospel at the top of their lungs - while still others rode the rails to hobo jungles.

Sit back and let me tell you some true stories about factory belles and ladies of the night, private eyes and literary con men, mediums and mesmerists, mystic medics and early crusaders against the "tobacco abomination." We'll experience adventures aplenty, including train wrecks, arctic exploration, stagecoach rides, seances, nudist colony raids and an 1875 balloon ascension.

When you have finished this book, I think you'll agree that in terms of its colorful heritage Michigan takes a back seat to no other state.

These articles originally appeared in *Encore* magazine during the period 1984-1990. I have rewritten some, corrected errors that came to my attention following the article's orginally publication and appended a list of my sources to facilitate further research and reading.

I want to thank Philip E. Schubert, editor and publisher of *Encore* for his support which helped me survive some rough times during the beginning of my career as a freelance Michigan historian - as well as for his friendship.

The cover illustration, representing Prof. Donaldson's balloon approaching the Michigan shore, is a water color by Judi Miller Morris of Allegan. Interestingly enough, Judi painted the scene from atop a remote fire tower in Wyoming where she worked during the summer of 1991.

My special thanks go to my wife, friend and partner, Priscilla, who constantly inspired me and performed the copy stand work and word processing, all the while keeping her sense of humor. Thanks also go to Judee Massie and Wally Massie who assisted greatly with computer work.

Larry B. Massie
Allegan Forest

Did Donaldson Jettison the Journalist?

Early balloonists often found themselves in a pickle.

𝕿 he dilapidated balloon, a veteran of many a carnival flight, skudded before the rising wind, some 30 miles out into Lake Michigan. Below, its rickety wicker basket skimmed the whitecaps, showering with spray its terrified occupants. It was about 7: 00 p.m. on July 15, 1875, and ace "aeronaut" Washington A. Donaldson and his passenger, *Chicago Evening Journal* reporter Newton S. Grimwood, having already dumped all their sandbag ballast, were clearly in a pickle.

Observing the balloonists' peril from a mile and a half away, the crew of a passing lumber schooner, the *Little Guide*, were in the process of bringing their craft about to come to the rescue. Suddenly, as if some heavy object had been cast from the basket, the balloon "shot upward to a great height, soon disappearing altogether from view." Although the crew gathered no further evidence, speculation soon centered on the probability that, the power of the press notwithstanding, Donaldson had jettisoned the journalist.

Amiable, athletic and known as a man who "could do anything he undertook to do, and would undertake anything that came his way," 35-year-old Donaldson had early in life taken to the stage as a gymnast, ventriloquist and magician. He toured the continent performing daredevil feats, appearing some 1,300 times during the period 1857-1871.

Fearless of heights, he took to the tightrope like a duck to water. In 1862, he walked across a canyon of the Schuylkill River in Pennsylvania on a rope 1,200 feet long, returned to the middle and finished his performance by jumping into the river at a height of 90 feet. Later he performed a similar stunt over the Genesee River gorge near Rochester, N.Y., on a rope 1,800 feet long, recrossing it while trundling before him a man in a wheelbarrow.

As awesome as were Donaldson's death defying feats of balance, by the 1860s they were being eclipsed by equally daring balloon ascensions, which, incidentally, were not dependent upon the existence of a fearsome chasm located near a population center. Invented by two French brothers named Joseph and Jacques Etiene Montgolfier, the first balloons were simply paper or cloth bags inflated with heated air. On September 18, 1783, the brothers placed a sheep, a rooster and a duck in the basket of one of their contraptions and watched the poor brutes ascend into the heavens. Fortunately those first living creatures to go up in a balloon landed safely in a nearby forest. That was more than could be said for many of the pioneer human aeronauts, who frequently plunged to their deaths.

Nevertheless the study of aeronautics and the intrepid scientists who engaged in aerial experiments increasingly captured the world's attention. By the 1850s the availability of gas used for illuminating purposes made ballooning somewhat less risky, although the cheaper to operate hot air balloons remained popular, particularly for carnival performers.

By that era John Wise had gained the reputation as America's leading aeronaut. On August 21, 1852, he performed the first recorded balloon ascension in Michigan. His gas filled craft, "Ulysses," rose from Detroit to a height of a mile and three quarters before safely landing in the vicinity of Pontiac. He described the sublime scenery he had observed during the flight as "the most beautiful sight I ever beheld and it is utterly impossible for the people who inhabit this region to conceive the real grandeur of their territory."

Not so fortunate was Michigan's first resident aeronaut, Professor Ira Thurston of Adrian, who was killed during a flight from that city in 1858. Other early balloonists who performed in Michigan included: Thurston's partner, W.D. Bannister, Professor H.L. Denniston, an aerial acrobat named Professor Pedanto, and Edward Lamountane. In 1873 Lamountane met an untimely end when he fell from a

Crowds gathered at county fairs to witness balloon ascensions.

height of half a mile, his body driving a six inch crater in the ground before the crowd that had assembled to witness the ascension at Ionia.

Despite such gruesome fatalities or perhaps because of them, ballooning continued to gain popularity as a spectator sport. Never one to shun the limelight, Donaldson was drawn inexorably to the air.

In 1871, he swapped all of his magical paraphernalia and one lesson in their use for his first balloon. Filling the big bag with "coal-gas" and without any training whatsoever, he succeeded in making an 18-mile flight only after he had cast off his coat, boots and hat to lighten the load. Six months later, while making an ascension from Norfolk, Va., the balloon burst open at a height of one mile. Clinging to the rigging, which descended with such "frightful velocity" that he "felt as though all my hair had been torn out," Donaldson landed in a chestnut tree, the limbs of which broke his fall. After crashing through the tree, he described his landing as "flat upon my back, with my tights nearly torn off and my legs, arms, and body lacerated and bleeding."

Undaunted, he next constructed "the Magenta," a state-of-the-art balloon holding 10,000 cubic feet of gas. He made several flights from Chicago in the Magenta, during one of which he was carried out into Lake Michigan and dragged more than a mile through the water until he was dashed unconscious against a stone pier.

Whether or not he was still suffering from the effects of that blow to his head when he conceived his next venture is uncertain. In any event, he teamed up with veteran aeronaut John Wise to test one of Wise's pet theories - that there is a constant current of air blowing from west to east at a height of three miles. If so, Wise conjectured, it should be a relatively easy task to zip across the Atlantic Ocean in a high flying balloon. The two convinced the *New York Daily Graphic* to put up the funding for the

A monstrous balloon for transcontinental travel designed by Thadeus Lowe.

construction of a gargantuan balloon weighing three tons and capable of being inflated with 700,000 cubic feet of gas.

But upon inspecting the monster, Wise wisely withdrew from the venture. Donaldson determined to carry on alone. After three unsuccessful attempts at inflation which burst the fabric, finally the gigantic globe stood ready for the flight. In lieu of a basket, Donaldson had rigged up a large life boat loaded with sand bags and provisions. He and two companions, named Ford and Lunt, cast off from a baseball field in Brooklyn on October 7, 1873, for what was to be an epic flight.

Just as Wise has suspected, the huge craft proved unmanageable. Fortunately it never made it out to sea. After traveling about 100 miles inland the aeronauts found themselves out of control, trailing along close to the ground amid trees and fences. Donaldson gave the signal to jump and he and Ford managed to escape with a few cuts and bruises, but Lunt was too late. Alone in the run-away monster and terror-stricken, he leaped at a passing tree but unfortunately plummeted through its branches to the ground, suffering mortal injuries.

Saddened but seemingly none the wiser, Donaldson, the intrepid aeronaut who seemed to have more lives than a cat, continued his balloon escapades. By 1874 he had won a national reputation as well as the honorary title of professor. Showman P.T. Barnum, always one to sense what the suckers would pay to see, soon offered him a position with his traveling circus, or hippodrome, as that master of hyperbole called it.

Barnum staked out his big tents on the Chicago waterfront in July, 1875. On the 14th, Prof. Donaldson made his first ascension, carrying several passengers. But the air was so still that the balloon only managed to get about three miles out over the lake. A ship towed it back to the starting point.

A *Harper's Weekly* artist sketched Donaldson's departure from Chicago on July 15, 1875.

Upon landing, one of the hippodrome managers took a look at the balloon and asked Donaldson: "What's the use of this? Why don't you go somewhere?" "Wait until to-morrow," he replied, "and I'll go far enough for you."

Nevertheless, on the following afternoon, with the wind blowing at 10-15 mph, Donaldson, according to Chicago newspaper accounts, appeared apprehensive about making his 138th ascension. Part of his reluctance undoubtedly stemmed from the condition of the balloon, which the papers observed "had been used in many other cities during the present season, and rents and patches all over its sides betokened rough usage and negligent repairs."

But, the show must go on. About 4:30 that afternoon as thousands of windy city residents cheered, the craft cast off. Donaldson waved from his perch in the rigging while Grimwood, who had won the dubious honor of accompanying him via a lottery held amongst the journalistic fraternity, gripped with white knuckles the sides of the gondola. The balloon gradually rose to a height of a mile or more, floated off over the lake and soon became but a speck on the horizon.

By 7:00 p.m. the aeronauts had suffered some unknown misfortune so as to place them in the dire straits observed by the crew of the *Little Guide*. They were the last to ever positively see the balloon. A hurricane strength storm which lashed Lake Michigan later that night further reduced the balloonists' chances of having survived.

Yet, the next day's newspaper accounts remained guardedly optimistic, speculating that the balloon had probably merely been carried a long distance by the storm.

Several ships that had crossed the lake to arrive in Chicago on the 18th brought disheartening news. A steam barge captain reported seeing a life preserver and something that looked like a basket floating about 50 miles northeast of Chicago. The captain of another vessel thought he saw "something like a balloon sticking out of the water."

And yet a third captain claimed he saw a dead body, wearing a gray coat, about 40 miles from Grand Haven. None of the seamen, however, had stopped to retrieve any of the flotsom.

Two days later came the startling news that the balloon had landed in the vicinity of South Haven. Unfortunately, upon investigation that proved the first of many false reports which would enliven newspaper reading throughout the summer. Spurred on by a $700 reward for recovery of the aeronauts' bodies numerous steam tugs began combing the lake - as the nation held its breath.

A week passed, then, miraculously, came news from the hereafter. A Dubuque, Iowa, medium, it seems, had established communication with Donaldson's spirit. It had requested he relay a message to the *Chicago Times:* "The balloon will be picked up and you will hear from it to-morrow. All hands are lost. Write to the *Chicago Times* and *Journal* that the balloon is lost and we are lost. Also that we threw out ballast supposing we were near the land, when we suddenly dropped into the lake and could not rise the second time."

To which the editor of the times quipped: "Air navigation becomes very discouraging business when the throwing out of ballast causes a balloon to fall, and it is no wonder that Donaldson was lost when so extra-ordinary an event took place."

Hard on the heels of the medium's message, bottles containing notes from the aeronauts began washing up on various beaches. On August 1, a workman claimed to have picked up a bottle on the lakeshore at Hyde Park, Illinois, bearing a barely legible note reading, "July 26- 2 a.m. - We cannot stay up more than an hour longer, as the gas is rapidly escaping. N.S.G." Weeks later another bottle was found away over on the Lake Huron shore near Port Hope, Michigan, containing a note which read: "Over Lake Michigan at 8 p.m. of the evening of starting, about thirty

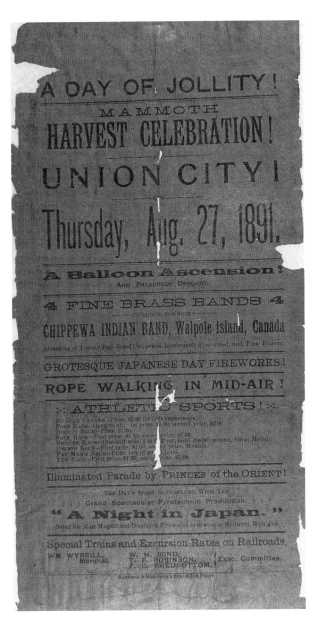

A DAY OF JOLLITY!

MAMMOTH

HARVEST CELEBRATION!

UNION CITY!

Thursday, Aug. 27, 1891.

A Balloon Ascension!
And Parachute Descent.

4 FINE BRASS BANDS 4
INCLUDING THE NOTED

CHIPPEWA INDIAN BAND, Walpole Island, Canada
consisting of Twenty Full-Blood Chippewas, handsomely Uniformed, and Fine Players.

GROTESQUE JAPANESE DAY FIREWORKS!

ROPE WALKING IN MID-AIR!

ATHLETIC SPORTS!

BICYCLE PARADE—Prize, $2.00 for best appearance.
FOOT RACE—Open to all; 1st prize, $3.00; second prize, $2.00
BIGGITY RACES—Prize, $3.00.
SACK RACE—First prize, $1.50; second prize, $1.00.
BICYCLE RACE—One-half mile; 2 in 3; First, Gold Medal; second, Silver Medal.
POTATO RACE—First prize, $1.00; second prize, 50 cents.
FAT MAN'S RACE—Prize, box of good cigars.
TUB RACE—First prize $1.50; second prize, $1.00.

Illuminated Parade by PRINCES of the ORIENT!

THE DAY'S SPORT TO CONCLUDE WITH THE
Grand Spectacular Pyrotechnic Production.

"A Night in Japan."
Being the Most Magnificent Display of Fireworks ever seen in Southern Michigan.

Special Trains and Excursion Rates on Railroads.

WM. WYRRILL, Marshal.

W. H. BOND,
T. F. ROBINSON,
J. C. SHEUBOTTOM,
} Exec. Committee.

KENDALL & ROBINSON'S STEAM JOB PRINT.

A broadside from a Union City extravaganza which featured a balloon ascension.

miles from Chicago and about three thousand feet high. A gale is coming from the north-east. The balloon is getting out of order, the gas escaping fast. Can't remain up much longer. Will surely land in the lake. Fearful storm. Donaldson."

Now, for that message to have gotten to where it was found, the storm would have had to have blown Donaldson's balloon, once lightened of Grimwood's weight, completely over Lake Michigan as well as the entire peninsula of Michigan. As far fetched as that seems, another nagging piece of information and one which might support that possibility, came on August 4, in the form of a letter from J.H. Stanwood of Algonac, on the St. Clair River. Stanwood wrote that he had observed Donaldson in the company of another young man walking the streets of his fair village. Having frequently seen the balloonist at Barnum's hippodrome in New York the previous winter, he was "positive of the identification." Donaldson had apparently shaved off his moustache but, wrote Stanwood, "the scar on his cheek rendered recognition an easy matter."

The plot thickened when the *New York Times* revealed the fact that Donaldson had instigated a false report of his death during a Philadelphia ascension the season before, apparently as a promotional gimmick. On the other hand, if he had actually pushed the journalist overboard and had somehow survived, had he not good reason for remaining incognito?

Any doubt as to the fate of Grimwood, was removed on August 17, when a body bearing his description washed up on the beach near Whitehall, Michigan. In his pockets were a Chicago Public Library card bearing his name and ironically, an autobiographical manuscript discussing his early ambitions to rise up in the world - that he had surely done, albeit briefly.

Periodically, other reports of sightings of Donaldson or the discovery of his body made the newspapers, but none

24

could be verified. Inevitably, the story became passe and such references were relegated to back pages, sandwiched among the ads for Castoria and magnetic trusses. By the following summer's gala centennial celebrations America had all but forgotten its fair-haired aeronaut.

Neither the balloon nor Donaldson's body were ever recovered. The fearless aeronaut had apparently used up the last of his nine lives - or had he?

Bitters, Balms and Bunkum: Michigan's Humbugs of Health

George Way's medicated ear drums were
found likely to produce permanent deafness.

Dr. Arthur J. Cramp, director of the American Medical Association's (AMA) special investigative task force, sat at his ponderous roll-top desk, letter opener in hand, intently examining the morning's pile of correspondence.

Suddenly the heavy silver-plated letter opener with a pair of naked cherubs on the handle clattered to the floor. Dr. Cramp reared back in his oak swivel chair and slapped both hands to his forehead. "Another patent medicine fraud in Michigan!" he groaned.

Since its founding in 1847, the AMA had labored long and hard to rid the profession of quackery. Over the years it battled an array of exotic-sounding medical theories.

Homeopathic practitioners prescribed drugs that produced on a healthy person effects similar to the patient's complaints. Allopathics dosed their victims with drugs that had the opposite effect. Eclectics let the patient, or next of kin, choose from either category. Thomsonians used only vegetable-based or "botanic" remedies in conjunction with a vapor bath. Hydropaths relied solely on the beneficial effects of copious gulps of water and various baths, showers, douches, and enemas. Periodically, other humbugs utilized magnetism, electricity, and clairvoyancy to dupe the ill.

A host of patent-medicine and mail order frauds also catered to those who preferred to doctor themselves. Across the country entrepreneurs intent on exploiting gullible sufferers bottled up elixirs, tonics, balms, and bitters guaranteed to cure everything from cancer to catarrh. From great cities and tiny hamlets flowed a stream of imaginatively named formulas whose chief active ingredients were alcohol, narcotics, or both.

Throughout the 19th century the AMA and legitimate physicians made little headway against patent-medicine rackets. The government's laissez-faire attitudes toward the rights of businessmen to make their fortunes insured a fertile ground for medical exploitation.

In 1905, muckraking journalist Samuel Hopkins Adams began an expose' of medical quackery in *Collier's* magazine. His series, "The Great American Fraud," focused national attention on medical con men and helped stimulate passage of the Pure Food and Drug Act of 1906. While that act did not prohibit harmful patent medicines, it did require proprietors to label ingredients and state the truth in advertising those products.

Government prosecution was slow at first. To speed up matters, Dr. Cramp developed and became director of the AMA's Bureau of Investigation in 1906. Until his retirement in 1935, he waged war on quackery by gathering information and publishing his findings in the *AMA Journal, Hygeia* and a series of pamphlets and books. Michigan, Dr. Cramp soon discovered, took a back seat to no state, not even to California, in diverse and widespread medical chicanery.

Detroit, incipient automobile capital of the world, claimed some dandies. George P. Way marketed a "medicated eardrum" his wife had invented. Fiendish rubber devices that resembled miniature toilet plungers were plugged into the ears. They "enabled a man who was so deaf that he could not hear thunder to hear the tick of a clock thirty feet away." The Way line also featured another "very unique instrument" that he had christened "Blowena" - a catarrh cure. The principal behind Blowena remains a mystery, but when Dr. Cramp examined the hard rubber eardrums, he concluded that if pushed into the ear they were likely to cause permanent deafness.

The Dae Health Laboratories of Detroit produced a less vicious but equally sham remedy. Newspapers nationwide featured full-page advertisements in which sports figures sung the praises of "Nuxated Iron." The product, a turn-of-the-century answer to "tired blood," was analyzed by Dr. Cramp, who reported that it contained little iron or any other ingredient of value.

"Nuxated Iron," baseball great Ty Cobb testified in 1914, "had filled me with renewed life and vigor" and resulted in his miraculous comeback at the age of 50. Cobb, by the way, did not turn 50 until 1936, eight years after he retired for good from baseball.

Jess Willard took "Nuxated Iron" and whipped Jack Johnson in 1915 and Frank Moran in 1916. Three years later, Willard found himself on the canvas for the first time in his career looking up at a new "tiger of the ring," Jack Dempsey. "Nuxated Iron," Dempsey announced, was also behind his stunning victory.

Willard evidently had failed to keep up his dosage. Dr. Cramp pondered what would have happened if both fighters had been taking the nostrum at the time of the match. "Would it have been a case of an irresistible force meeting an immovable body?"

But Detroit bunkum was nothing compared to what was going on outstate. The center of medical fakery seemed to be southwest Michigan. Kalamazoo, Battle Creek, Jackson, and Grand Rapids boasted substantial quack empires. Local boosters dubbed Marshall "patent medicine town" in honor of the 32 different drug companies that operated there over the years. Wayland, Albion, Hastings, Otsego, Coldwater, and many other smaller communities also supported one or more medical-hokum hucksters,.

Why a disproportionate number of medical con artists operated out of southwest Michigan is open to conjecture. Perhaps the inventive turn of mind and entrepreneurial daring that brought success via turkey feathers to the Warren Featherbone Company of Three Oaks, a fortune based on petticoats to ex-blacksmith John McLarty of Kalamazoo, and established the Marshall-based Brooks rupture supporter dynasty also spurred a host of get-rich-quick medical scams. Or maybe it was the influence of St. Luke's Hospital in Niles.

While researching his series on fraudulent medicine,

muckraker Adams had noted diplomas from St. Luke's Hospital hanging on the walls of many of the bogus doctors he visited. St. Luke's, Adams discovered, was a diploma factory where quack doctors purchased authentic-appearing certificates entirely in Latin complete "with your name handsomely engrossed in an old round hand style of letters, with two pieces of dark blue ribbon and a large corporate gold seal affixed thereto." Those who wanted to become a "doctor" could purchase the document on "Heavy Royal Linen Paper" for five dollars or on "Imitation Parchment" for $7.50. The top of the line"Genuine Sheepskin" model ran 10 dollars.

Since its founding in 1896, St. Luke's Hospital had yet to admit its first patient. A local doctor got wind of the scheme and brought it up at a meeting of the Michigan State Board of Health in 1899. The board found that no Michigan law compelled the institution to have patients or prohibited it from selling diplomas. The state legislature soon remedied that situation. St. Luke's president, Dr. Charles Granville, faced personal travail about the same time the new law went into effect. One of his several wives discovered his whereabouts, and he suddenly skipped town for parts unknown.

St. Luke's co-founder, Dr. Arthur Probert, also received bad tidings in the form of extradition relating to certain medical chicaneries practiced on the good people of Bourbon, Indiana. St. Luke's Hospital closed its doors, and "Doc" Probert and "Doc" Granville moved their printing press and font of Latin type to Chicago, where for a brief time their "Christian Hospital" continued to market bogus credentials.

While some fraudulent doctors relied on phony sheepskins to bamboozle patients, others coined imaginative titles to lend legitimacy to their swindles. A.W. Van Bysterveld of Grand Rapids earned his dubious livelihood as an "Expert Inspector of Urine." Van

Van Bysterveld Medicine Co., Ltd.

A. W. Van Bysterveld

Expert Inspector of

URINE

17-19-21 Sheldon Street
GRAND RAPIDS, MICHIGAN

Van Bysterveld boasted he had "spent a lifetime in examining human urine."

Bysterveld, whose portrait reveals a curly-haired, middle-aged gentleman with a rather villainous uplift to his moustache, boasted he had "spent a lifetime in examining human urine," an average of 25,000 specimens a year.

Once clients learned of Van Bysterveld's exotic services in newspaper ads, they simply mailed in a vial of their urine labled with their age and sex. The Expert Inspector sent back a description of what ailed them and supplied weekly medicinal doses at a healthy fee. Since contemporary bottles were stoppered with corks, one wonders about the reaction of the Grand Rapids postal employees who had to handle Van Bysterveld's mail.

Van Bysterveld's expertise, he informed clients, had originated in a "careful and secret process handed down generation after generation, and most carefully guarded by the old families of Europe." In 1910 Dr. Cramp gave the litmus test to Van Bysterveld's methodology. AMA chemists prepared a mixture containing tap water, a trace of pepsin and ammonia, and a little yellow dye for color. Cramp sent identical vials of the fluid from addresses in Illinois, Iowa, and Michigan to the "urine expert." Back came the following diagnoses:

Diagnosis one: "Careful examination of the urine shows there is too much acid in the blood, which will cause a rheumatic condition, the back is weak, and you will have a tired nervous feeling most of the time."

Diagnosis two: "Careful examination of the urine shows the circulation of the blood to be very poor, the liver is not working properly, which will cause gas in the stomach and bowels and will effect (sic) the heart. You have caught a little cold which has settled in the back and stomach, and you will have a nervous feeling."

Diagnosis three: "Careful examination of the urine shows you are losing too much albumin in the urine, which will cause the back and kidneys to be weak, and there is a catahrral condition of the stomach and bowels, and you will have a tired nervous feeling most of the time."

Evidently the only condition common to three individuals, secreting a mixture of water, pepsin, yellow dye, and a trace of ammonia was a nervous feeling. Then again, a certain degree of nervousness seemed advisable for anyone dealing with Van Bysterveld.

Dr. Cramp hoped that "the overworked fraud-order department of the United States Post Office will in the near future get around to this picturesque, but vicious, humbug," and that Van Bysterveld be treated to free board and lodgings at the Michigan State Penitentiary.

Jackson , site of the state prison, already boasted a ring of medical charlatans who dwelt, not behind bars, but at fashionable downtown addresses. Using a complicated system of interlocking directorships, they buncoed mail-order patients from coast to coast and across the Atlantic. J. Lawrence Hill, A.M., D.D., M.D., lent his numerous medical credentials to a fraudulent tuberculosis cure but only held ten percent of the share in the corporation. The major stockholders and principal officers of the Hill Consumption Cure were a notorious band of medical rogues.

F.L. Childs, vice president of the outfit, had quit his job as salesman for the Upjohn Company to become proprietor of a Kalamazoo-based mail-order constipation cure called "Pomola." "When the Hill concern got into trouble over testimonials for its treatments, the majority of which came from people who were dead, Childs authored a new set and signed them as "an anxious seeker after health."

The secretary and treasurer of the Hill Consumption Cure, a Jackson lawyer named F.C. Badgley, when not busy in the courthouse served as president of two other fraudulent operations. His Magic Foot Draft Company marketed a plaster mass which, when applied to the bottom of the feet, supposedly sucked out the poisons that produced rheumatism. Rheumatic patients in America and England stumped around with thick wads of plaster on their soles for months. Dr. Cramp's team analyzed the magic drafts and found no curative elements whatsoever.

Badgley also distributed to his patients pills containing methylene blue. He promised that consumption of those "Magic Regulators" caused the kidneys to release pent-up rheumatic poison. Patients could "rest assured that the Magic Regulators were doing their work" if their urine turned light blue. Since methylene blue produced this effect on any healthy person, needless to say, the regulators usually did their work.

Lawyer Badgley's other firm, the Van Vleck Pile Cure Company, was founded by G.W. Van Velck. From 1887 until 1891, Van Vleck had operated a Cincinnati diploma mill, the "Medical University of Ohio," which sold diplomas from ten dollars to $500 apiece. Van Vleck not only filled the offices of president and dean of the university, but also served as the entire faculty. In 1891 he was arrested and tried for felonious fraud.

Van Vleck's partner, William Hale, another notorious quack, fled the state and set up practice in Denver as a Chinese physician, "Dr. Gun Wa." Indicted in U.S. district court for fraud, Hale skipped to England, where the bobbies nailed him and he spent 18 months in "gaol." By 1900 Hale was running a "British Medical Institute" in Jackson. Two years later, the institute folded when he suddenly left town just ahead of a warrant. Nevertheless, Hale continued to practice his shenanigans on an international scale. In 1914 Dr. Cramp located him in Mexico as the proprietor of "Los Medicos Ingles." As late as 1922, "Hale's Epileptic Relief" pills guaranteed a cure for "fits and epilepsy." Hale's tablets were found to contain nothing more than strong laxative properties.

To return to the roster of J. Lawrence Hill's Consumption Cure Company, R.A. Oliver served as treasurer and also owned a quarter interest in the Magic Foot Draft concern. H.H. Mallory, advertising agent for Hill, had originally

34

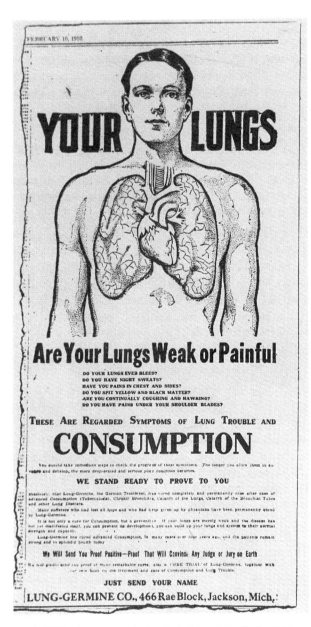

A 1910 ad for one of Jackson's numerous medical scams.

been vice president. He also served as vice president for the Magic Foot Draft and Van Vleck Pile Cure companies, which, incidentally, shared the same offices at their London branches in England.

The Magic Foot Draft Company operated an extensive printing plant in Jackson. Dr. Cramp noted a certain "typographic sameness," to much of the advertising material sent out by the Hill, Van Vleck, and Magic Foot concerns.

The three firms practiced similar sales techniques as well. Respondents to extravagant advertising claims received a free trial package of worthless nostrums. The Consumption Cure included, for example, the Ozonal Lung Developer." It was a hard rubber tube containing a wad of cotton saturated with sassafras, peppermint, and eucalyptus oils. Air sucked through the developer was described as "more heavily charged with oxygen than if breathed otherwise." The kit cost ten dollars, more than the average weekly salary at that time. Those who did not bite got a follow-up letter in a month. The next plea reduced the price to five dollars and finally three dollars. Not only were the drugs worthless, Dr. Cramp testified, but likely to complicate genuine medical problems.

Another consumption cure, dubbed "Lung Germine" because it had been discovered by an "old German doctor scientist," also came out of Jackson. The firm's medical director, C.R. Wendt, M.D., claimed to be a graduate of Leipzig University in Germany. Authorities at the university, however were unable to locate Wendt's name among their records. The Lung Germine people practiced marketing hijinks very similar to the other bogus Jackson firms. Wendt added a vaguely worded but nicely printed certificate of guarantee with each order. On analysis Dr. Cramp found Lung Germine to belong to the family of patent medicines he termed "bracers." The mixture consisted of water, a dash of sulfuric acid, and sherry wine fortified to bring the alcohol content up to 44 percent, or approximately the same as a jigger of Jack Daniels.

J.W. Brant of Albion took advantage of the public's thirst for medicinal toddies to turn out Brant's Soothing Balm. Brant proudly labeled each bottle as 98 percent alcohol. His balm was a veritable panacea, good for "bowel complaints, rheumatism, neuralgia, tooth and ear aches, and scalds, bruises, and sprains." Sufferers could quaff the soothing balm or rub it on the smarting parts. Brant also assured his remedy was good for "colic in horses."

In addition to his booze balm, Brant marketed Wheeler's Nerve Vitalizer as a cure for all nervous diseases. Brant, urged delicate run-down women, in particular, to tone up their exhausted nervous systems with four doses a day of his vitalizer. Actually the elixir contained large quantities of sodium bromide and potassium bromide, which are depressants.

From Coldwater came Dr. C.D. Warner's White Wine of Tar Syrup. It contained no tar and very little wine, but a generous helping of opium. E.H. Ryno of the Allegan County community of Wayland, proprietor of Ryno's Hay Fever and Catarrh Remedy, received a $100 fine when government chemists found his substance to contain 99.95 percent cocaine hydrochloride. The cocaine was not illegal, but Ryno had failed to note its presence on the label.

On the other hand, F.A. Stuart of Marshall gulled the public with a different recipe. "Stuart's Catarrh Tablets" contained 60 percent cane sugar, a touch of starch, and a generous helping of ash. The government could detect little therapeutic value to those ingredients and slapped the tablet-maker's wrist with a small fine.

Stuart's Calcium Wafers, he claimed, cured constipation, eradicated skin eruptions, and cleansed impure blood. The compound contained no poisonous ingredients and children could "take it with freedom and their delicate organisms would thrive with its use." But when a 16-month-old

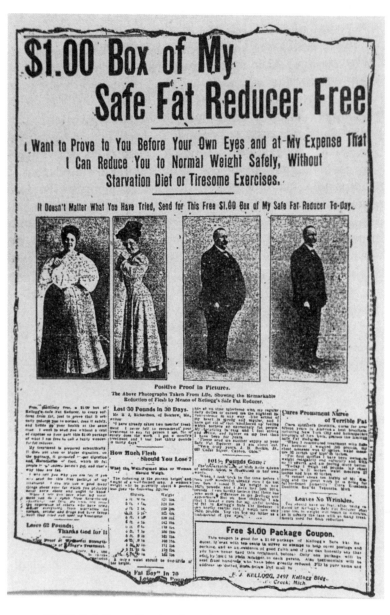

"Anti-Fat" Kellogg offered embarassing competition to the more reputable Battle Creek practicioner, Dr. John Harvey Kellogg.

child in New Hampshire swallowed a few of the wafers he was seized with convulsions and died. Analysis of the nostrum revealed a substantial quantity of strychnine.

In Battle Creek, the Kellogg name had been prominent since 1876, when flamboyant Dr. John Harvey Kellogg took over as superintendent of the Battle Creek Sanitarium. Kellogg had earned genuine medical credentials, but through the years he walked a tightrope over accepted medical practices with his unique mixture of hydrotherapy, colon hygiene, and the health foods he invented, such as nut butter, caramel cereal coffee and corn flakes. As Dr. Kellogg struggled to keep his name clear, an unrelated namesake offered embarrassing competition. Frank J. Kellogg, or Anti-Fat Kellogg as he was called locally, made a fortune on a phony obesity cure composed of toasted bread crumbs, thyroid gland, and poke root.

The Old Indian Medicine Company of Battle Creek duped the sick with generous-sized bottle of "Wa-Hoo Bitters." Charles Kent Wilson's panacea offered a sure cure for malaria, catarrh of the stomach, neuralgia, and St. Vitus's dance. Consumers did a Wa-Hoo dance of another type. The product contained a generous amounts of epsom salts and a strong laxative plant drug.

The "Cereal City's" T. Gorham extensively advertised his Home Treatment For Catarrh. Catarrh, an obsolete term for any sort of cold or sinus infection, was naturally a common complaint. Gorham scared readers with the possibility of catarrh turning into asthma or tuberculosis. Those who ordered his remedy got for five dollars a small bottle of worthless brownish liquid for internal use and a one-ounce tin of petroleum jelly for "swabbing out their smeller." Gorham also conducted a lucrative sideline. He sold his original letters written by asthma sufferers to other patent medicine crooks. In 1911 he marketed those he had received over the previous two years -13,000 of them!

Kalamazoo entrepreneurs took advantage of their city's reputation as the world's leading producer of celery to invent a variety of celery-flavored nostrums. Patent-medicine proprietors discovered that the crunchy vegetable contained a substance ideal for quieting "nervous disorders." James Farnum mixed up batches of Kalamazoo Celery and Pepsin Chewing Gum. The Kalamazoo Medicine Company concocted Celery Pepsin Bitters, and the Quality Drug Stores marketed Kalamazoo Celery and Pepsin Bitters. The Hall Brothers,Fred and George, specialized in Celerine Compound. To make their product more effective, they took the liberty of adding alcohol and cocaine to the mixture. Other Celery City medicine-makers capitalized on celery's reputation as an aphrodisiac to come up with a cabinet full of sexual elixirs.

As the century wore on, increased government prosecution and the AMA's relentless campaigning made heavy inroads into Michigan's quack industry. By the time of his retirement in 1935, Dr. Cramp counted far fewer of the diabolical frauds that killed and maimed victims, and he had shifted to exposing harmless, albeit bogus, obesity cures, cosmetics, and deodorants. Yet, the closets of more than one prominent family continue to hold patent-medicine skeletons. Now medical chicanery is a thing of the past. Right?

Travelers in Time: Early Tourists Describe Michigan

Father Pierre Charlevoix, who visited the site of Niles in 1721.

𝕱ather Pierre Charlevoix summoned his faithful spaniel for an after-supper walk along the St. Joseph River downstream from the future site of the city of Niles. It was a hot August evening in 1721. Charlevoix and his faithful Indian companions had canoed down the east coast of Lake Michigan from Michillimackinac. Their mission was to locate a water passage to the great sea that was supposedly off to the west somewhere.

Charlevoix tossed a stick into the river and his dog jumped in after it. Back at camp, the Indians heard the dog's splashing and, not knowing the good priest was out for a stroll, interpreted it as the sound of a deer swimming the stream. Two braves set out with loaded muskets. One of them, being a "clumsy fellow," was sent back to camp. The other spotted a silhouette - the black-robed padre in the dusk - and, mistaking him for a bear standing on its hind legs, crouched down and prepared to fire his load of three musket balls.

At that point, Charlevoix, fortunately, called out. When he reached the hunter, struck speechless by what had almost happened, Charlevoix realized how close he had come to permanently ending his journey on the banks of the St. Joseph. Such were the perils of 18th-century travel in what would ultimately become the state of Michigan.

Charlevoix's travel narrative, first published in 1744, is one of the earliest of a genre that provides valuable insight into the history of the region. The day after his brush with death, Father Charlevoix arrived at Fort St. Joseph near the site of present-day Niles. He found the fort unimpressive, merely the house of the commandant, "a trifling thing surrounded by a poor palisade." A settlement of Potawatomi resided near the fort and across the river lay a village of Miami Indians.

Charlevoix sojourned over five weeks at Fort St. Joseph before continuing his travels via the St. Joseph-Kankakee portage, the Illinois River, and down the Mississippi to its mouth. He spent much of that time among the two Indian tribes encamped on the St. Joseph River. The erudite Jesuit recorded choice information concerning their customs in his journals.

He found that Potawatomi and Miami braves occupied themselves with sports and games of various sorts while the squaws did most of the camp chores. Major sporting events included intertribal lacrosse matches that lasted for days.

Charlevoix paid a visit to the chief of the Miamis, a tall, "well-shaped" man who had had the misfortune of losing his nose during a drunken brawl. While the priest was there, a delegation of Potawatomi arrived to play a game of straws. The teams divided 201 short straws into piles of ten each and one pile of 11. Each player then picked a pile and he who got the 11 won a point. Naturally, to make the game more interesting the braves gambled over the results. The play at this aboriginal casino on the St. Joseph continued day and night until some braves were completely naked. With nothing else to wager, the losers returned home.

Charlevoix also described another game which he felt had "almost always bad consequences with respect to their manners." It was the Indian version of a 1990s singles bar. The young braves of the tribe erected a circle of wooden posts and the band set up with their tom-toms, flutes, and rattles in the middle. A packet of different-colored down feathers was placed on top of each post.

The village belles adorned themselves with their favorite colored down and gathered for the festivities. As the band struck up a number, the young Indians danced around the posts. Periodically a beau would grab a handful of the same colored down that his sweetheart wore, sprinkle it on his hair, dance around her, and whisper sweet nothings in her ear concerning a later rendezvous. Charlevoix noticed that despite the utmost vigilance of mothers, the couples always

A 1724 engraving of Indians playing a game of chance.

44

managed to slip away to "their place of assignation."

A century later, when another traveler recorded a visit to Niles, Christian missionaries had put an end to that pagan tomfoolery. William Hypolitus Keating, a member of a government expedition sent to explore the sources of the Mississippi in 1823, published an account of his adventures the following year. En route from Fort Wayne to Chicago, Keating's party took a dog leg detour to visit the Baptist Indian mission at Niles.

The ancient Potawatomi village where Charlevoix had witnessed the gambling party had long since disappeared. On its site, Issac McCoy had established a missionary school in 1822. The Carey Mission, named after a celebrated Baptist missionary to India, sought to acculturate local Potawatomi children in the ways of the white man.

Keating found four student dormitories, a schoolhouse and a blacksmith's shop, all built of logs. Forty to 60 pupils lived at the mission. McCoy's philosophy, in contradiction to the usual missionary ventures, was to first civilize his flock, then convert them to Christianity.

In addition to the "three R's," boys studied agricultural arts and manual trades, and girls received further instruction in spinning, weaving, sewing, and the like. The students had also succeeded in clearing, fencing and planting 40 acres of Indian corn. Nevertheless, the little academy had been forced to tighten its collective belts that spring due to the loss of a wagon load of flour from Fort Wayne that had upset in fording the Elkhart River. What's more, the students had been deprived of milk because the cows had gotten into a patch of wild prairie onion, and that had ruined the taste of their milk for weeks.

The Carey Mission had been established as one of the conditions of the 1821 Treaty of Chicago. In exchange for about five million acres of land comprising most of southwest Michigan, the Potawatomi received a few paltry payments, the Carey Mission and little else. McCoy soon realized that his plan could have little success as long as traders and white settlers plied his students with firewater. In 1830 he moved his mission to Kansas and a segment of the Potawatomi followed. During the late 1830s, President Andrew Jackson reneged on the various treaties and his Indian Removal Act called for the trans-Mississippi evacuation of the tribes. By 1840 all but a few isolated bands of southwest Michigan Indians had been rounded up by federal troops and herded west.

The Michigan Territory, created out of the Northwest Territory in 1805, had been bypassed by earlier settlers largely because of a prevailing notion that it was a huge swamp. Within a few years after Keating made his visit to the Carey Mission, however, pioneers began filtering into the region. Reports of the lush soil they encountered and the completion of the Erie Canal in 1825, which facilitated travel from Buffalo to Detroit, spurred a land rush into the southern tiers of counties in the late 1820s and 1830s.

By the early 1830s, two east-west roads crossed southern Michigan. The "Chicago Military Road" ran from Detroit to Ypsilanti and then south through the southernmost tier of counties to Chicago, roughly equivalent to today's U.S. 12. The "Territorial Road" branched off at Ypsilanti and continued through the second tier of counties approximately paralleling the present route of I-94. Towns sprung up along these routes, as thousands of settlers traveled west to stake out homesteads in southwest Michigan. Stagecoaches also carried curious tourists, who frequently penned accounts of their travels.

In September of 1833, two British authors, making a sweep of the United States, climbed aboard a stagecoach drawn by four horses in Detroit and set out for Chicago. They had not made each other's acquaintance and, British reserve being what it was, they spoke scarcely a word to each other during the journey. Both, however wrote books

In the 1830s hordes of travelers found primitve lodgings at taverns such as Thompson's, near Dearborn.

about their travels when they returned home.

Patrick Shirreff, a farmer by trade, took special note of Michigan's agricultural prospects. He found the general aspect of the land disappointing, thought the soil looked poor and judged Michigan's park-like oak openings to be infertile. The houses were "mere log huts."

When Shirreff arrived in White Pigeon on the third day of his journey, he found more to his liking. The broiled ruffed grouse served for breakfast in the hotel there raised his spirits. He thought White Pigeon a "small, pretty village, comprised of well-painted frame-houses," and called White Pigeon Prairie "one of the most beautiful and fertile prairies in Michigan." Perhaps the whole territory had gotten its reputation for fine land from this one section, he mused. A fellow passenger, an old New England farmer on his way to Illinois, remarked, "Surely, this must have been the place where Adam and Eve resided."

Aloft and disdainful of most things American, Shirreff comes across in his book as a rather unpleasant individual. While traveling across Ontario, he had noticed a wasp's nest and, being of an experimental turn of mind, tried to get a traveling companion stung so he could observe the consequences. His friend refused to oblige. With some degree of pleasure, the reader of Shirreff's narrative learns that at White Pigeon, a wasp stung him on the eyelid, enabling him to personally compare the relative properties of Michigan and British insects.

When they reached Niles, the travelers exchanged their coach for an open wagon which was better able to negotiate the rest of the miserable road to Chicago. They took on another passenger, a farmer from Nottawa Sepee Prairie, located adjacent to the Indian reservation in Kalamazoo and St. Joseph counties.

The farmer was en route to Chicago where another Indian treaty was scheduled for negotiation. It seems that he had let his hogs run loose in the woods all summer, a common frontier custom, and when he rounded them up, he was 20 shy. He blamed the Indians for losses that were more likely caused by wild animals, disease, or other settlers. Nevertheless, he fully expected to get payment for the whole number from the Indian agent.

Joseph Latrobe, the other British author on board the stage, was headed for Chicago to view the negotiations with the Potawatomi. His perceptions of the Michigan landscape were entirely different from Shirreff's. Latrobe had never beheld "a more lovely undulating country, covered with rich grass, interspersed with forests or groups of trees, and varied by limpid lakes."

At Chicago the Indian commissioners and agents made short work of the Potawatomi. Chief Leopold Pokagon signed the Chicago Treaty of 1833 that relinquished several million more acres of ancestral land, including the site of Chicago itself. Apparently the Michigan hog farmer and others caught the ears of the commissioners and the Potawatomi also lost the Nottawa Sepee Reservation. The small payments guaranteed in the Chicago Treaty of 1833 went delinquent until Chief Simon Pokagon, Leopold's son, pressured Congress half a century later and secured $150,000 compensation that was still due the tribe.

An American writer, who would win critical acclaim for his work, made a trip on horseback across the state in December of 1833. Charles Fenno Hoffman, a 25-year-old New Yorker, went on his wintry tour of the west, curiously enough, for health reasons. He took the Territorial Road to Marshall where he stayed overnight at a recently constructed inn. The walls of the hotel had not yet been plastered, but Hoffman noted that the well-stocked tavern "wore already the insignia of a long established inn in an old community." A placard alerted residents of a town meeting to promote the development of a railroad. It would be another dozen years before the Michigan Central Railroad actually linked Marshall with civilization.

Hoffman liked Kalamazoo County "as much as any part of Michigan I have seen." He stopped briefly at Comstock where "the enterprising young gentleman after whom the place is called," Horace Comstock, had created a flourishing establishment containing " a frame store, several log cabins, and two or three mills." Little did Hoffman or Comstock realize but these entrepreneurial dreams were doomed to failure, thanks largely to a decision to locate the county seat at a rival little settlement called Bronson.

Hoffman bypassed Bronson, which would become Kalamazoo in 1836. Instead, he made his way across windswept Prairie Ronde to the more prosperous village of Schoolcraft. The half-frozen traveler quickly located the scene of major activity, the village tavern. The warm room held what Hoffman called "a salad of society." He shared a round of cocktails with a "long haired 'hoosier,' a couple of smart-looking 'suckers' from the southern part of Illinois, a keen-eyed leather-belted 'badger' from the mines of Wisconsin, a 'red horse' from Kentucky," and a native Wolverine dressed in a white capot, Indian moccasins, and a red sash.

Hoffman found the little community, clustered at the edge of the big woods in the center of Prairie Ronde, much to his liking. The richness of the prairie soil and the ease with which it was cultivated gave the residents, he thought, ample leisure for many recreations. Villagers enjoyed their favorite sport, fox hunting on horseback with full packs of hounds. Other sportsmen followed the thrills of wolf, bear, and badger-baiting, in which a disabled wild animal was pitted against a pack of dogs. Schoolcraft prided itself on the "number of fine running horses, blooded dogs, and keen sportsmen it has in proportion to the population." Alas, Schoolcraft, which like Comstock had vied for the county seat, would also never realize its ambition of becoming the dominant metropolis in the area.

In the summer of 1836, a cultivated English authoress

Harriet Martineau, four decades after she braved a trip across pioneer Michigan.

traveled across Michigan by stagecoach. Harriet Martineau took the Chicago Military Road and experienced some of the worst travel conditions imaginable. The road was atrocious - muddy and full of sink holes. Frequently, passengers had to walk alongside the stage. Near Jonesville, they ran over a hog wallowing in the road.

The road west from Jonesville got worse and in places was "absolutely impassable." The stage driver detoured through a swamp that offered better footing and meandered through a blazed beech forest. A full day's drive accomplished only 42 miles. It was dark when the exhausted travelers arrived at an inn near Sturgis. The hostelry was already filled with travelers. Mrs. Martineau waited three hours for supper. Adults curled up in corners of the dining room, and 16 children slept across chairs or on the floor. The English lady was fortunate to be allotted a stuffy "little closet whose door would not shut."

The going improved the next day, "the best roads since New York State," she called them. The travelers made it all the way to Niles without having to walk once. The authoress waxed poetic over the beauty of the passing scenery, a "wilderness of flowers, trailing roses, enormous white convolvulus, scarlet lilies, and ground ivy. "Milton must have traveled in Michigan before he wrote the garden parts of Paradise Lost," she gushed.

A traveler from Rochester, New York, recorded a similar impression of southern Michigan scenery in 1841. Lansing Swan went by stage over the northern route to visit relatives near Kalamazoo. En route he "passed through the most beautiful country I ever saw, the ground all along the road richly ornamented with wild flowers and dotted with crimson by the thousands of strawberries which cover it everywhere." The stage driver drove as he wished, through the oak openings or on the road depending on the terrain. The village of Kalamazoo had prospered since Hoffman's 1833 ride. Swan liked "its location and general appearance better than any I have seen."

After a visit with relatives, Swan headed for Niles where his brother lived. He stopped for the night at Sumnerville in Cass County. The only available accommodations at the inn were an upstairs room, already occupied by the local "school marm." Frontier customs being what they were, Swan slept with the teacher. He didn't seem to mind the inconvenience. Since she went to bed first and he got up first, both escaped embarrassment.

Swan left Niles for his return trip home via the old Chicago Military Road, "a great turnpike," he thought. At Adamsville he ate "a miserable breakfast, got up by good-looking, but outrageously dirty women, who, I should think, were Hoosiers." He fared better at the next stop, the Sturgis Prairie Hotel, where he enjoyed an "excellent dinner, warm cakes, tea, bacon, and eggs." Nevertheless, Swan summed up his visit to the Wolverine State thusly: "But for ugly-looking women, Michigan assuredly excels, as well as dirty taverns and good-looking school marms."

The Reverend James L. Scott, a Seventh-Day Baptist missionary, recorded an even worse impression of southern Michigan. Returning from an extended journey to the west in 1842, Scott traveled across Michigan on horseback. "I was as much disappointed in Michigan as any country I ever saw," he wrote. To the reverend's eye, "the water and visage of the inhabitants were very indicative of an extremely unhealthy climate." He passed through a small village near Coldwater that had been "almost depopulated by the unflinching hand of death."

Fever had ravished the area to such an extent that Scott had never seen such "desolation and devastations." He blamed much of the illness on poor drinking water. Near Centreville, his thirsty boy had taken a drink from a barrel used for domestic purposes. The water was so vile it made him violently ill for days. The Reverend Scott was only too happy to leave Michigan behind.

By 1846 travel across the lower peninsula had improved. The Michigan Central Railroad reached Kalamazoo that year and, as the first locomotive tooted into town on a Sunday morning, every church in the village emptied into the street.

George Augustus Frederick Ruxton, a British adventurer returning from a tour of the far west in 1846, penned one of the earliest descriptions of travel on the Michigan Central. After boarding the train at Kalamazoo, he found the railroad "a very primitive affair, with but one line of rails, which in very many places, were entirely divested of the iron, and in these spots the passengers were requested to 'assist' the locomotive over the 'bad places.'" Nevertheless, "after killing several hogs and cows," the train arrived safely in Detroit.

In 1852 the Michigan Central finally reached Chicago. Improved tracks as well as cattle guards made train travel more reliable as increasing numbers sped across Michigan by rail. Lillian Foster, a writer from New York City, traveled over the Michigan Central in June of 1855 and thought the towns along the route, "gems, spots of earth upon which the eye can feast." She got an excellent dinner in Marshall "conducted with such order, taste, and decorum" that she imagined herself in a fashionable hotel.

Kalamazoo proved so irresistible that Foster tarried three days. As she toured the village she saw "residences, neat and tasteful, surrounded with grounds filled with shrubs and flowers." Kalamazoo pioneers, unlike most other frontier settlers, had left many of the original trees standing. Kalamazoo had by this time taken the nickname "Burr-Oak Village" in honor of its magnificent foliage. Foster observed the view from Mountain Home Cemetery and looked out upon "a city with tall spires, nestled in a deep woods."

A decade later Philip Mason, an Indiana physician, set out on a genealogical tour of southern Michigan. From Grand

W.G.Jackman.N.Y.

Philip Mason, an Indiana doctor who toured Michigan in the 1860s.

Rapids he took a stage over the Plank Road that ran to Kalamazoo. It stopped at the Junction (now Plainwell), so named because it was at the intersection of the plank road and the highway to Allegan, to have an axle repaired. He then continued the bone-jarring ride over the worn planks to Kalamazoo.

Mason, as revealed in his autobiography, was somewhat eccentric. His religious beliefs, for example, ran toward Spiritualism. While in Kalamazoo he took a drive out Asylum Avenue to the state hospital where he enjoyed a lengthy tour. The next day he visited the county poor farm, formerly the site of a short-lived communal experiment called Alphadelphia. He left Kalamazoo for Jackson, where he inspected the state prison. Dr. Mason, apparently, was covering all bases concerning a potential future residence.

Archibald Porteous, a Scot, arrived in Kalamazoo in 1889 to visit relatives. He noted the extensive celery fields cultivated by Hollanders and which had earned Kalamazoo its new nickname, "Celery City.' Porteous could not determine if the name, Kalamazoo, was of Indian or Dutch origin. The double row of shade trees that flanked the city streets impressed the visitor, as did the brick business district and residential neighborhoods filled with "white villas with green Venetian shutters and porches where whole families sat out in the evening."

A resident proudly asked Porteous if he did not think Kalamazoo was the prettiest place in America. While he had only been to a few American cities, Porteous admitted that it was "one of the prettiest towns he had yet visited." He was surprised to open the *Kalamazoo Gazette* the next morning to read this item: "Mr. Archibald Porteous, of Glasgow, Scotland, who is on a tour in America, and is at present visiting his brother, whom he hasn't seen for forty years, is said to have expressed the opinion that Washington and Kalamazoo are the two most beautiful cities on this continent." The fact that neither Porteous nor his brother had yet reached 40 troubled him more than the hyperbole.

Porteous found one thing rather disturbing about Kalamazoo - its many railroad crossings. He was amazed to find "at least thirty level crossings within a mile of the post office." Trains ran across the main streets, and streetcar lines, roads, and foot paths were "intersected at random by railroads."

Which just goes to show that despite the evolution in transportation we have seen in 170 years of travel narratives, nearly a century later some things stay the same. Or perhaps you have never waited at a train crossing in Kalamazoo?

Michigan's Literary Rogues: They Stole, Swindeled, Gulled and Bamboozeled - and Then Wrote Books About It

SHORT STORIES & SKETCHES OF CONVICT LIFE

RESULTS OF THE LIFE OF CRIME
VERSES, SONGS, Etc.

The cover of "Billy the Yegg" Butler's 1916 autobiography revealed his fate.

$\mathcal{B}$illy the Yegg" Butler and his gang made one big mistake when they knocked over a certain Benton Harbor jewelry store in 1899. They underestimated the Michigan "rubes" and failed to plan their getaway. Butler, recently released from a five-year stint at Sing Sing, should have known better.

Following a lead from a "goat" who had spotted the set-up, the gang blew into town on the train about three o'clock one afternoon. Each checked into a different hotel and later that night they met to plan the heist. Early the next morning they sawed out the lock on the door to the rear of the store, drilled the big old-fashioned safe, and "loaded her up and touched her off." They netted a sack of money, diamonds, and other valuable stones.

Unfortunately for them there was no early morning train out of Benton Harbor. They determined to foot it out of town. Heading south, they got lost and after a long weary hike were nabbed with the goods on them by the Elkhart police. That caper cost Butler a five-year sentence in Jackson, meted out by a Benton Harbor judge.

There is nothing particularly remarkable about Butler's long criminal career which, incidentally, eventually earned him a life sentence in the Kentucky State Penitentiary. But what separates him from thousands of other recidivists is that he wrote about his exploits in a pamphlet entitled *Behind Prison Walls: The Story of a Wasted Life*, first published in 1916. By thus plying his pen, Butler joined a select group of literary rogues including the likes of old Sile Doty; "Yellow Kid" Weil; Chicago May, "The Queen of Crooks"; William Davies, the super tramp; and J.P. (Gyp) Johnston. All had one thing in common - they wrote books describing how they stole, swindled, conned, gulled, and otherwise bamboozled in Michigan.

The crown of Michigan knaves goes to Sile Doty. Born in St. Albans, Vermont, in 1800, Doty's earliest and fondest recollections were of stealing his sibling's toys. By 1834, when he emigrated to Adrian, Michigan, he had carved out a reputation as "the most-noted thief and daring burglar of his time."

Highlights of his many exploits, which he brazenly and unrepentedly described in an autobiography posthumously published in 1880, include robbing members of the Michigan legislature in their hotel rooms in Detroit, routinely providing household necessities for his family and neighbors by "stealing from the rich and giving to the poor," and horse-filching campaigns conducted throughout Michigan and bordering states, Canada, New England, and even the continent of Europe. In 1837 he committed a memorable foray into Kentucky, returning with a string of fine horse flesh and a young slave to boot.

While not above burglarizing any opportune prize as well as committing an occasional murder, Doty gained his greatest fame as a horse thief. An 1837 caper illustrates his typical *modus operandi*.

He had settled down that spring on a farm near Tecumseh in Lenawee County to try his hand at legitimate work for a change. But the memory of a certain prize set of black horses belonging to a Detroit hotel keeper haunted him day and night. Unable to resist the temptation any longer, he set out that summer to get his hands on that team.

A friend in Detroit cased for him the barn where they were kept and one night about 11 p.m. Doty unlocked the barn door with the set of master keys he never left home without. Quickly saddling one of the horses, within minutes Doty was racing across the countryside leading the other. By daybreak he had holed up at another friend's home in Washtenaw County.

There he made "the grievous mistake" of laying over for two days instead of one. The owner of the horses had sent out posses in every direction. Doty discovered this four miles south of Adrian when five mounted men rushed him.

Sile Doty, horse thief par excellance.

He jumped from his horse and ran into a dense woods where he managed to lose his pursuers.

But Doty was not about to give up that easy. He shadowed the posse to an Adrian tavern. While they downed a few drinks in celebration of their success, Doty crept up to where they had tethered the horses and was soon off again. Eventually he sold the team in Ohio and returned to his farm $225 the richer.

Despite his daring and skill Doty did occasionally get caught. His career was temporarily interrupted by several short vacations in Jackson Prison. But by 1851, a Lenawee County judge had had enough of the old scoundrel. Thinking him 53 years old, he sentenced him to 17 years, a term he thought sufficient to keep him out of circulation the remainder of his scriptural life span of three score and ten. It was not.

Doty, in fact, found a way to continue to steal within the prison walls and even to gain entry to the female department when the mood struck him. For some reason, prison officials released him two years early for good behavior. Before death finally sneaked up on the 76-year-old outlaw, he managed to serve additional two and four-year sentences for burglary and horse stealing and to write his unabashed autobiography.

A tad less flagrant a scamp than Doty, but probably one guilty of a greater gross take, was J.P. Johnston. Not only was he a truly great gyp artist, he was undoubtedly the most prolific of the literary rogues. Johnston detailed his success in separating suckers from their cash in *Twenty Years of Hustling*, published in 1888, and a long series of sequels including, *What Happened to Johnston, How to Hustle*, and *Grafters I Have Met*. Not content with getting the public to buy books describing how he gulled them, he added insult to injury by periodically issuing the same books under different titles.

Auctioneering was Johnston's forte and he used a full

J.P. "Gyp" Johnston auctioning off shoddy goods in the Upper Peninsula

63

complement of ploys, including the bait and switch, shills, paid testimonial givers, and quick getaways to foist shoddy goods at big prices. But he usually stayed within the letter of the law, as it was written during the 19th century anyway. Michigan proved fertile soil for his shenanigans.

During one memorable tour throughout the state he ranged all the way across the Upper Peninsula, a route most con men considered suicidal. Johnston rode the train north, stopping off at likely-looking towns. Pushing a special two-wheeled cart loaded with trunks containing his stock to the center of town, he would mount his portable stage and soon attract a crowd with a fast-paced spiel such as:

"Now, ladies and gentlemen, the first article I am going to offer for your inspection is a fine silver-steel blade knife with a mother-of-pearl handle, brass-lined, round-joint tapped, and riveted tip-top and bottom, a knife made under an act of Congress at the rate of $36 per dozen. There is a blade for every day in the week and a handle for your wife to play with on Sunday. It will cut cast iron, steam, steel, wind, or bone and will stick a hog, frog, toad, or the devil and has a spring on it like a mule's hind leg and sells in the regular way for. . ."

He sold knives, soap, underwear, socks, furniture polish and patent medicine, and in the excitement of the bidding got many times the normal retail value. In Houghton he chanced upon an opportunity to buy a lot of fire-damaged merchandise, including water-soaked rolls of cloth. He cut that nearly worthless material into standard bolts 16 2/3 yards long and talked a crowd of men into buying them at two dollars apiece. Pretending not to know the true value of the material, he guaranteed that if the men's wives were not satisfied, they could trade the cloth for two dollars worth of other goods.

Just as planned, the next morning a crowd of disgruntled wives "large enough to fill a small circus tent" awaited him. He cheerfully soothed their anger by exchanging the bolts for other merchandise, auctioned off at his highly inflated prices, of course. When Johnston returned south on September 1, "as it had begun to get cold up there," he had amassed a roll of more than $3,000.

Johnston found the pickings so good in Michigan that he frequently returned there from his headquarters in Chicago. One day while auctioning at the Michigan State Fair being held in Jackson, a stranger approached Johnston, asking him for a loan of $25. It seems he was flat broke and needed that sum to get his sideshow in operation. The show featured a fat woman, a dwarf, an albino, and a Circassian girl (a Russian race known for its frizzy hair). Johnston said he would stake him providing they split the profits.

The man took Johnston to his hotel and introduced him to his wife, two sons, and daughter. Johnston asked where the show people were. "I have introduced you to all of them," he replied.

"But where is your fat woman?" Johnston demanded. The man pointed to his wife. "Why, Great Heavens," Johnston shouted, "she is an thin as a match and as long as a wagon track; how are you going to make her fat? And the Circassian - where is she?"

The man pointed to his daughter, whose hair was all done up in tin cans and who told him, "Never mind about the show! Everything will be all right." At one o'clock, they were at their tent, ready for business. As Johnston recalled: "The fat woman was in her long silk robe and as big as a hogshead. The dwarf was in his swallow-tailed coat and wearing a plug hat, and his face deeply furrowed with wrinkles. The albino boy had white hair and the Circassian girl had her dark bushy hair standing out in all directions from her head. The albino played the fife, the dwarf the snare drum, the Circassian lady the cymbals, and the fat woman the bass drum."

The sideshow hoax which separated suckers from their cash in Jackson.

That band, a big canvas painted with caricatures of the "Greatest of Living Curiosities," and the barker' fast-paced banter drew large crowds throughout the fair. The farm folks eargerly paid their admission to go inside the tent for a closer look at the living curiosities and no one complained. At the fair's end the fraudulent freaks split a profit of $600 with Johnston.

Johnston wrote his wife to "get herself and their little boy ready to start at a moment's notice, as I was liable to send for them very soon and start a circus of our own."

Not all Michigan scams were being run by non-residents, however, as William H. Davies, the super tramp, found out. Davies had immigrated to America from Wales in 1895. Practically destitute, the 23-year-old soon fell in with a notorious professional begger called Brum who taught him the art of tramping. Davies learned to beg from door to door, how to hop a freight car, the fellowship of the hobo jungle, and above all that - honest work was to be performed only as a last resort.

Davies, Brum, and another tramp known as Australian Red rode the rails west into Michigan. Winter was setting in and Brum had one more trade secret to show his young apprentice. They disembarked at a certain small town, a southern Michigan county seat. Unfortunately it was unnamed in the book Davies' published in 1908, titled the *The Autobiography of a Super Tramp* .

The trio of tramps calmly waited at the depot for the approach of the village marshall. Within 15 minutes they saw him coming, his bright star gleaming on his breast . Brum told the others to let him do the negotiating.

"Boys," said the marshall, "cold weather for traveling, eh?"

"We don't feel the cold," Brum replied.

"You will, though," advised the marshall, "this is but the beginning, and there is a long and severe winter before you, without a break. You would certainly be better off in jail. Sixty days in our jail, which is considered one of the best, if not the best, in Michigan, would do you no harm, I assure you."

"As for that," Brum dickered, "we might take 30 days each providing, of course, that you make it worth while. What about tobacco and a drink or two of whiskey?"

"That'll be all right," agreed the marshall, "here's half a dollar for a drink, and the sheriff will supply your tobacco.

"No, no" said Brum, "give us a dollar and three cakes of tobacco, and we will take 30 days, and remember, not a day over."

The marshall handed them a dollar bill and three cakes of chewing tobacco and told them to go to Donovan's Saloon on the main street. He would see them later in the day, at which time, he told them with wink, "you will be supposed to be just a bit merry."

As the bums headed for the saloon, Brum explained the scam. The marshall got a dollar for everyone he arrested, the judge three or four dollars court costs for every conviction, and the sheriff a *per diem* fee of one dollar for every prisoner he boarded. The officials were all in cahoots and the taxpayers unknowingly funded a place for tramps to spend a nice cozy winter with plenty to eat.

Later that afternoon, the boys began whooping it up. The marshall arrested them for being drunk and disorderly and conveyed them to the jail. There the sheriff greeted them: "Welcome, boys; you want the 30 days and 30 you shall have, no more or less, and you will be none the worse for it, I promise you, at the end of the month."

He ushered them into a homey day room where 30 or 40 other vagabonds greeted Brum. "Have you seen Detroit Fatty?" asked one. "Or the Saginaw Kid?" asked another.

The next morning they were taken before the judge who sternly told them, "I do not see why peaceable citizens should be disturbed in this way by drunken strangers." He

Hobos who rode the rails in the 1890s sometimes spent
comfortable winters in Michigan jails.

fined them each seven dollars and court costs, or 30 days in the county jail. They took the jail time and spent a pleasant month of rest and relaxation.

Following which, the trio moved on to several other Michigan county seats where similar situations existed, and thus they passed the cold winter of 1895-96. They spent the following summer berry picking in the St. Joseph vicinity and then moved on to Chicago where they soon blew their entire season's savings on a memorable drunken spree.

Davies continued to follow the life of a hobo for the next six years until he suffered the misfortune to fall while hopping a moving train. He lost a leg in the accident. Davies returned to Great Britain where he launched a respectable literary career, producing highly-acclaimed poetry and a series of autobiographical volumes.

Crooked county officials, as described by Davies, were apparantly quite numerous at one time in Michigan. "Yellow Kid" Weil, one of America's most notorious and flamboyant con-men, whose exploits, incidently, provided the basis for the movie, *The Sting*, described another Michigan caper in his autobiography published in 1948. The Yellow Kid operated mainly in Chicago, periodically making a foray into Michigan. In 1933, for example, he stung "Uncle Jake" Kindleberger, paper magnate and founder of the city of Parchment, to the tune of $15,000. Decades before that, however, he found a way to make big money off of worthless Michigan land.

By the turn of the century the Michigan resort communities located along Lake Michigan's eastern shore had become a vacation mecca for Windy City citizen. Hordes of wealthy Chicagoans eagerly bought up Michigan land. Weil determined to take advantage of that fact.

He bumped into a Chicago character known as Colonel Porter, who was practically penniless but acted the part of a retired Texas millionaire. Porter, as Weil discovered,

70

had a cousin who owned thousands of acres of worthless cut-over swamp and dune land near Hart in Oceana County. He was also the Oceana county clerk and register of deeds. Weil sent Porter up to have a little talk with his cousin.

The cousin readily sold them a large tract of the land at the going price of a dollar an acre. He also agreed to increase his normal fee for recording deeds from $2 to $30, which he would split with Weil and Porter. Thus the Elysium Company was formed.

Weil had a large map drawn up of the tract, designating sites for a sprawling clubhouse, golf course, tennis courts, and swimming pool. The remainder of the land was platted into thousands of standard-sized lots. He installed Porter in a nice downtown Chicago office furnished with a beautiful panoramic view of the nonexistent resort. Next he had printed an expensive-looking brochure describing the vacation paradise.

But none of the lots were for sale. Weil simply gave them away to prosperous acquaintances whom, he told, he would like to have as neighbors in the private Elysium resort. Weil carpeted Chicago with deeds to Oceana County property, advising each grateful recipient to get their deed registered as soon as possible. Many were shocked at the exorbitant registration fee but, after all, they had gotten the land free. Few ever inspected their worthless holdings, until it was too late. Even then there was nothing they could do; the deeds were legitimate and had not been sold to them.

After two months Weil withdrew from the venture, having netted a profit of $8,000 as his share. Occasionally, however, he found himself being chased down the street by one of two burly Chicago detectives he had inadvertantly swindled with Elysium lots. But, as Weil wrote in his autobiography, "I was fast on my feet and they never caught me."

It would be tempting to add to the roster of literary

The cover of "Gyp" Johnston's popular account of his life as a con-man.

crooks the names of Austin and George Bidwell, who perpetrated a one million pound forgery on the Bank of England in 1872. The Bidwell borthers had grown up in Grand Rapids and Muskegon before moving to New York City. But unfortunately the fat autobiographical volumes each of them produced following their parole from Newgate Prison in 1884 contain no mention of depredations committed on Michigan soil.

Instead let us leaven the list with a light-fingered lass from the land of the limerick, Chicago May, "the queen of crooks." Born in 1876 near Dublin, Ireland, pretty auburn-haired May Churchill began her life of crime at the age of 13. She robbed the money box in her father's bedroom and "flew the coop with sixty pounds.' A few weeks later she walked down the gangplank in New York City. Alone and without any real destination, it did not take her long to get hooked up with a set of hoodlums. Fond of partying and generous with those she liked, May proved affable enough, but when angered she displayed a well-developed case of the legendary red-headed Irish temper. Her underworld friends taught her criminal techniques at which she became very adept. Drifting west she became 'a prize graduate of the Chicago School of Crime," hence her moniker. She did her post-graduate work in New York, London, and Rio de Janeiro.

May became a highly touted call girl, but not in the usual sense of the term. In May's own words, "it was very seldom that a John ever got as far as being intimate with me." Instead May usually took her victim out on the town for a good time, got him good and drunk, and picked his pockets good and clean in the process. On occasion she resorted to knockout drops or an accomplice, but usually her innocent winning ways did the trick.

By 1924 May was no spring chiicken - her tough life, to say nothing of 15 years of assorted jail terms, had taken their toll. That year she took up residence in Detroit. The

"Motor City" was booming, with "money being made and money being spent." May figured that what she lacked in youth and energy she "more than made up in the cunning of experience."

Let May describe a typical evening's work in her own unique style:

"One day I went down Park Boulevard and picked up a swell guy in a car. Before we got very far I had taken his leather. We were parked near a gasoline station. Up comes a Ford law car. Two burly bulls jumped on us. I had presence of mind enough to put the wallet into the John's outside coat pocket. They scared the poor sucker so badly that he ups and tells them he was taking me to a hotel and had promised to give me ten dollars. Both of us were taken to the police station, and that was my first arrest in Detroit."

May got out of that scrape by convincing the judge, "a good decent Irishman," that she was a hard working, respectable woman whose husband had deserted her with two small children. But the sun was setting on May's long career of crime. She got pinched a couple more times in Detroit and was sent to prison for violating probation. While there she nearly died from the effects of a long delayed operation.

Just when it looked like May was finally down and out one day a good-hearted bull "put the bug into her head" to try to write for a living. Her autobiography published in 1928 sold well enough for her to start a new life. But in it she commented: "Crime never occured to me as sin. I only want to reform now, from a business point of view."

Whether May or any of the other line-up of literary rogues ever actually reformed is debatable. Most had a hard time concealing the glee with which they recalled their villainous exploits. Perhaps their literary labors were one last attempt to extract money from suckers in a more legitimate way.

Chicago May, "the queen of the crooks."

As to their veracity, many of the crimes they described can be documented in other, more reliable, sources. But then again, perhaps the caveat offered by Yellow Kid Weil says it best: "Truth is cold, sober fact, not so comfortable to absorb. A lie is more palatable. The most detested person in the world is the one who always tells the truth, who never romances."

Communists on The Kalamazoo

PRIMITIVE EXPOUNDER.

"Then opened Jesus their understandings, and expounded unto them in all the Scriptures."

Vol. II.   ALPHADELPHIA, MICH. JUNE, 12, 1845.   No. 15.

THE PREACHER.

ORIGINAL.

TEST OF DISCIPLESHIP.

BY J. EATON.

" By this shall all men know that ye are my disciples, if ye have love one to another."—St John 13: 35.

On that ever memorable night that witnessed the betrayal of our divine Lord and Redeemer into the hands of his murderous enemies by the traitor Judas—when he was about to take his leave of that little band of disciples which he had gathered around him during his brief but glorious ministry on earth, he gave them this important criterion by which men might know whether they were his true disciples, or whether they were his only in name. Yes, in that last discourse which he delivered to his disciples before his crucifixion, when he was about to leave them and ascend to his Father and our Father, we find the language we have selected for our text. "By this shall all men know that ye are my disciples if ye have love one to another."

This is a true criterion: one by which men may know, in all ages of the christian church, who are and who are not the true disciples of Him who was the brightness of the Father's glory, and the express image of his person.— In the verse preceding our text, he says, "a new commandment I give unto you, that ye love one another, as I have loved you, that ye also love one another." If they followed the examples of their Master, an observing world would know that they were his disciples; but if they walked counter to his examples, it would be known that they were in truth none of his, however loud their professions might be. Says an Apostle, "if any man have not the spirit of Christ, he is none of his."

The brief but eventful history of Christ's ministry on earth delineates a character worthy of imitation. Did he love that little band of disciples who had forsaken their all, and enlisted in his cause ? Yes, he loved them, and as he loved them, he commanded them to love one another. Was his love confined within the narrow circle of those few followers who delighted in listening to his teachings, and to obey his precepts ? No, no. Did he love his friends, and hate his enemies ? Did he pray for his friends, and invoke the curses of high Heaven upon his foes ? No, indeed; such was not the character of the immaculate Son of God. Shall we limit that love that glowed in the bosom of the world's Redeemer ? It encircles the whole creation of God's intelligences. He had love for all however sinful they might be. Yes his love was universal, and he embraced many an opportunity to instill the heavenly principle of universal love into the hearts of his followers.

Hear him in that best of all sermons, on the Mount, giving instruction to his disciples.— " Ye have heard," said he, "that it hath been said thou shalt love thy neighbor, and hate thine enemy: but I say unto you, love your enemies," &c. He assured them that by so doing they would be the children (characteristically) of their Father which is in heaven, for he dispenses his blessings alike upon the evil and the good. If, therefore, we would be the disciples, of the Son of God, we must love, not only our friends, but our enemies also : for thus are we taught by his precepts and examples. Yes, it is the duty of every professed disciple of Christ to manifest the spirit of their Master by loving all, both friends and foes.

We think it will not be unprofitable, dear friends, to examine professors of Christianity by this infallible criterion given us by our Savior in the text, that we may know who are, and who are not his disciples. We deem

They were not wild-eyed revolutionaries or long-haired hippies. They were practical-minded pioneers used to hard work and discipline. But they were communists none the less. And in 1844 they banded together to put their distinctive social theories to the test. For nearly four years, hundreds of members lived a utopian dream they called Alphadelphia, located on the Kalamazoo River just west of Galesburg.

The concept of Utopia - the perfect society - can be traced as far back as Plato. Each succeeding age translated the assumption of man's goodness and perfection into a literary model which reflected that generation's own temper and problems.

Sir Thomas More's *Utopia* (1516) provided a name for the phenomenon. Francis Bacon's *New Atlantis* (1622) offered an Elizabethan version. By the 18th century, radical Protestant sects began attempting actual utopian experiments on the cheap land available on the American frontier. At Ephrata, Pennsylvania, and at several Shaker and Moravian communities religious-oriented societies moved from the planning into the demonstration stage.

In 1805, a German communitarian sect under the leadership of Father George Rapp established a colony at Harmony in Beaver County, Pennsylvania. In 1814, the Rappites migrated farther west to the banks of the Wabash in Posey County, Indiana, where the founded Harmonie. It survived for a decade, but feeling they had ventured too far into the wilderness, the Rappites sold their property to Robert Owen. Owen, a self-made Scottish philanthropist and social reformer, launched an experiment that first demonstrated the secular possibilities of communism. His New Harmony inspired a wave of similar experiments throughout the1820s in New York, Pennsylvania, Ohio, and Indiana.

Meanwhile, the chaos of the French Revolution had spawned a number of utopian socialist thinkers including

Entienne Cabet, Henri de Saint-Simon, and Charles Fourier. Fourier (1772-1837),a mad mathematician, became the wildest and perhaps the most influential of the French socialist reformers of the first half of the 19th century. In his first book, published in 1808, Fourier outlined his novel philosophy. He believed the earth to have a life of 80,000 years, half of "ascending vibrations" and half of "descending vibrations." He saw his age as the last of the ascending stage, and the world would soon move into the era of "harmony." The age of harmony would bring a number of marked changes in the natural world, such as: the aurora borealis would somehow distribute great warmth to the northern regions, lions would become beasts of burden, whales would pull ships across seas consisting of a delicious lemonade, and six live moons would replace the present natural satellite.

Fourier's attraction lay not in his bizarre cosmology but in his new theory of social organization. He would channel the various facets of human nature into a harmonious system.

Model communities comprising 1,620 persons of various categories would be constructed so that man's dysfunctional traits such as the "butterfly" passion, which led men to desire a change of activity, and the competitive and intrigue passions could be harnessed for the good of society. Fourier's ideal colonies, known as Phalansteries, would be self sufficient little cities. A huge Phalanstery building would provide for group living under one roof and community meals. A new code governing relationships between the sexes would legalize "free love." Plenty of time and energy would be reserved for cultural activities but work would remain important and its products would be distributed 1/3 to capital, 1/4 to talent, 5/12 to labor. Soon, Fourier's scenario ran, 2,985,984 Phalansteries would surplant all other forms of social organization.

In the early 1840s, such American reformers as Horace

Greely and Albert Brisbane popularized Fourier's ideas and launched a second wave of communal experimentation. Antebellum America also witnessed an era of religious and social ferment. This golden age of reform gave rise to movements promoting abolition of slavery, women's rights, temperance, health reform, and imaginative new religions. Avant-garde women eschewed corsets to don shocking bloomer outfits . Sylvester Graham advocated vegetarianism and left the graham cracker as a legacy. Phrenology, which taught that bumps on the head revealed a person's character, swept the country, and traveling phrenologists read "cranial developement" before packed houses. Orson Fowler, a prominent phrenologist, also designed octogon houses for healthier living.

Joseph Smith founded the Mormon church, spiritualism popularized spirit rappings, table tippings, and ouiji boards, and in 1844 thousands of hysterical Millerites slipped on Ascension robes and gathered atop nearby hilltops to await the Judgement Day. At a time when practically everyone embraced some aspect of the outre', Fourierism met ready acceptance.

The 1840s saw at least 25 Fourierist societies established in America. Some, like Brook Farm, located near Boston, won permanent fame due to the participation of transcendentalist authors. But most were short-lived failures. Michigan's sole Fourierist experiment began under the aegis of Dr. Henry R. Schetterly.

Schetterly, a physician in New York state, had moved his family of five to Ann Arbor around 1840. He soon became prominent in local scientific and educational circles and published a Universalist oriented journal, the *Primitive Expounder*. Schetterly fell under the sway of Brisbane and Greeley and became an enthusiastic advocate of Fourierism. Intensely idealistic, Schetterly grasped the concept of communal living as a panacea for the greed and oppression

Members of a successful New York state commune, the Onieda Community, engage in a work bee.

he saw around him.

Schetterly first launched a campaign to promote his new found theories through the columns of the *Primitive Expounder.* Then on December 14, 1843, he called a convention to consider the formation of a Michigan Fourierist phalanx. Fifty-six delegates from Kalamazoo, Oakland, Wayne, Washtenaw, Genesee, Jackson, Eaton, and Calhoun counties assembled in a schoolhouse in Columbia Township near Jackson. For three days they debated from early morning to midnight, hammered out a rough constitution, and appointed a committee of three, including Schetterly, to view three potential sites for their domain. The first Michigan Fourierist phalanx would be called Alphadelphia - meaning "First Brotherhood." The convention adjourned, agreeing to reassemble in three weeks at Bellevue in Eaton County.

One of the potential sites for Alphadelphia lay just west of Galesburg in Comstock Township. Schetterly and his committee arrived December 23 to inspect the land and get a feel for local attitudes toward the experiment. Schetterly, a charismatic speaker, spent three days visiting with Galesburg families. He described in glowing terms the possibilities for a better life the new brotherhood would bring, relating visions of Arcadian healthfulness, of a pastoral life full of happiness and mutual comfort, of a Utopia on the banks of the beautiful Kalamazoo River. The local pioneers responded en masse to his persuasive rhetoric and anxiously sought admittance to the brotherhood.

While it now seems unlikely that pioneers, known for practicality, shrewdness, and independence, would so quickly fall for such a proposal, actually pioneer lifestyle was in many ways similar to socialism. The hard life on the frontier, with few neighbors and scarce tools, inspired a cooperative approach. Settlers routinely loaned farm implements, draft animals, and food as the need arose. Barn raisings, threshing bees, and corn huskings not only got the work done efficiently but served as social gatherings. The sense of community that already existed among the pioneers, where everyone scraped for a living, was actually not far removed from what Schetterly advocated.

By December 27, Schetterly could write his fellow Fourierists that in Galesburg "an ardor now exists among the people in this place for entering into association which never can be cooled until their wishes shall have been realized." When the convention reassembled in Bellevue on January 3, 1844, Schetterly reported that about 3,000 acres of farmland had already been offered to the association. He enthusiastically described the lay of the land:

"The Kalamazoo river, a large and beautiful stream, nine rods wide and five feet deep in the middle, flows through the domain. The mansion and manufactories will stand on a beautiful plain, descending gradually toward the bank of the river, which is about twelve feet high. There is a spring, pouring out about a barrel of pure water per minute, half a mile from the place where the mansion and manu-factories will stand. Cobble-stone more than sufficient for foundations and building a dam, and easily accessible, are found on the domain; and sand and clay, of which an excellent brick have been made, are also abundant. The soil of the domain is exceedingly fertile, and of great variety, consisting of prairie, oak openings, and timbered and bottom-land along the river."

The 51 delegates soon voted Comstock Township as the site for Alphadelphia and then turned to perfecting their constitution. The finished document contained a number of liberal provisions, such as: "The religious and political opinions of the members are to be unmolested and inviolate; and no member shall be compelled to support in any way any religious worship."

Members who fell ill were to be provided for out of the

The communal dining room at the Onieda Community, an experiment similar to Alphadelphia.

common fund. Any male 21 years of age, of good moral character, and who had "six months provision for the future," could become a member by a two-thirds vote of the existing membership. Females could become members at the age of 18 and their labor and skill was to be considered equal to that of males. Free education would be provided for all children.

The association was set up somewhat like a stock venture. Members who qualified relinquished their land, tools, and personal effects. These were appraised by Schetterly and members were issued stock valued at $50 per share. One-quarter of the profits from the sale of manufactured goods and agricultural products would be distrtibuted proportionately to each member's stock. All members would work an eight-hour day at a suitable task and receive a uniform wage.

By March of 1844, more than 1,100 men, women, and children had become Alphadelphians. By May, the membership had risen to 1,300. With many others clamoring to join, the association began to worry about too sudden growth and rejected further members at that time. The association had secured deed to 2,814 acres of land, 927 under cultivation, at a cost of $32,000, mostly in stock. It began turning down other offers of land so as not to create too heavy a tax burden.

During the spring of 1844, the Alphadelphia domain on the Kalamazoo River hummed like a gigantic bee hive. Scores of farmers, millwrights, machinists, furnacemen, printers, mechanics, and skilled paper and cloth makers arrived to ply their specialized trades for the good of all. The Alphadelphians soon dug a mill race, set up a saw mill, and erected a two-story wooden "mansion," 20 feet by 200 feet in size. Some members continued to live on nearby farms and reported for work each day.

By the following spring, the society had erected a wagon shop, a blacksmith's shop, and some barns. Children crossed the Kalamazoo River by boat to attend school in a log building on the south side of the river. Schetterly continued to publish his *Primitive Expounder* as a Universalist journal and started up a secular organ, *The Alphadelphian Tocsin.* The brotherhood sold hides, baskets, wheat, barley, rye, and livestock. The first year's efforts showed a profit. With plans to soon build a larger mansion, a seminary, and a public library, the future looked bright for Kalamazoo County's Utopia.

No records survive to document everyday life at Alphadelphia but there is every reason to believe that the residents practiced the routines outlined by Fourier. If so, each member worked at a task suitable to his or her training and disposition. When one job grew tiresome, another was selected. Fourier advocated changing tasks every few hours. He also thought children, who naturally enjoyed playing with mud pies, were ideal for the community's dirtier jobs.

As might be expected from a diverse population living under one roof, some members' eccentricities jarred on other's nerves. Teacher James Allen Knight loved to play his violin for hours on end. But the occupant of an adjoining room, "Avery the Shaker," failed to appreciate the endless strains of music. A bit of poetry that appeared in the "Alphadelphia Tocsin" suggested his predicament:

The Fiddler's Lament
Oh Allen, oh Allen, how you do torture me,
Surely you'll kill me dead as a stone;
All the while sawing, and rasping, and scraping
Surely you'll scrape all the flesh from my bones.

History has failed to record how the Shaker and the teacher resolved their differences, but it is certain that their problem and other problems involving basic human nature were the undoing of the Alphadelphia experiment.

By 1846, though still running in the black, the association was in trouble. One old Alphadelphian remembered the disgruntling fact that "too many large families, poor and hungry, who could do no work, or were incapable of supporting themselves, got among us and were a continual expense - a hole in the meal bag from first to last..."

The Alphadelphians were strong on theory, had more than enough land and plenty of labor, but there was little money coming in. The lack of available capital produced unemployment and its consequent demoralization. The quality of the food declined to the point where buckwheat cakes comprised practically the sole staple.

Schetterly later summed up the situation: "All lived in clover so long as a ton of sugar or any other such luxury lasted; but before provisions could be raised, these luxuries were all consumed, and most of the members had to subsist on coarser fare than they were accustomed to."

The officers exasperated matters by selling some outlying farms too cheaply. Members began withdrawing, claiming back their land and possessions, and the situation worsened. Laborers became discouraged and left. Influential members spent the winter elsewhere, and when they returned "everything was turned up-side-down."

Alphadelphia struggled on into 1848, then totally broke up as each member tried to salvage something. Some lost nearly everything while a few managed to make a little profit. P.H. Whitford, who had been married at Alphadelphia in 1845, remembered with good humor that he "went into the association with a yoke of oxen and came out with a wife and a buggy."

After the demise of Alphadelphia, many former members remained in the Galesburg vicinity and eventually made good via the capitalist system. Others wandered away to seek their fortunes elsewhere. Schetterly remained a stead-

"COME ALONG AND HELP DIG THEM TATERS!"
"WHY, YOU MUST BE A NEW COMER IN THIS PHALANSTRY, OR YOU WOULD KNOW THAT I BELONG TO THE EATING GROUP."

A cartoon from the 1840s ridiculed Fourier Socialist experiments like Alphadelphia.

fast Fourierist a while longer.

He joined the La Grange Phalanx in Indiana. When it collapsed, he journeyed to the Wisconsin Phalanx at Ripon, but in 1850 that association also broke up. Eventually Schetterly gave up his idealistic quest and secured a job as a government lighthouse keeper in Grand Traverse Bay. By 1860 he had recouped a small fortune and the former socialist was prosperous enough to keep a maid.

Kalamazoo County purchased a 173-acre tract of the main Alphadelphia domain in February of 1849 for the sum of $3,000. It became the county farm - the old folks home - where indigent senior citizens and, in the 19th century, the insane suffered out their last days. Samuel Durant's 1880 *Kalamazoo County History* records that the original two-story Alphadelphia mansion still served as the farm residence.

A century after the Alphadelphia Society had broken up, its last remaining vestige surfaced when a 500-pound bell that had once summoned the association members to meetings was found collecting dust in a barn. During the experiment's heyday, it had hung in the belfry of the great mansion. After the mansion was dismantled, the bell served the Galesburg Fire Department for decades before its replacement by a siren.

The 20th century brought the abandonment of the concept of the county farm and the conversion of the property into a park. Today, beautiful River Oaks Park, the site of a colorful yet little known incident in Kalamazoo County's history - where communists once attempted a noble experiment in social reform - offers recreation to a society that has achieved an ease of life and a standard of living little dreamed of by the Alphadelphians.

One old pioneer remembered that he "went into the association with a yoke of oxen and came out with a wife."

Allan Pinkerton and the Mystery of the Tell Tale Boot Prints

Allen Pinkerton's trademark was emblazoned on the covers of his many accounts of detective adventures

$\mathcal{A}$llan Pinkerton, America's original "private eye," stopped dead in his tracks. There before him in the mud was the exact set of bootprints for which he had been stalking the streets of Adrian, Michigan, for weeks. They had been left by a distinctive set of English-made boots marked by double rows of round-headed nails in the soles and heels and a heart-shaped design in the center.

Pinkerton had finally struck a "hot trail," a set of tracks he strongly suspected would lead him to a railroad robber and murderer.

Born in Glasgow, Scotland, on August 25, 1819, Pinkerton fled to America in 1842 to avoid imprisonment because of his involvement in Chartism, an outlawed, revolutionary, democratic movement. The muscular young Scot, who knew how to use his fists as well as his head, eventually settled near Chicago. Elected deputy sheriff of Kane County in 1846, he subsequently became Chicago's first detective. He established his own private detective agency there in 1850. Within a few years he had established a national reputation for his bulldog determination and sleuthing skills.

In early 1854, U.S. Postmaster General James Guthrie summoned the detective to Washington. Guthrie informed Pinkerton that he had no one in the department with detective skills. There were plenty of politicians hired via the spoils system, but none that he could trust.

He wanted Pinkerton to undertake a special assignment and devote his entire attention to it. It seems that there had been a rash of mail robberies on the Michigan Southern and Northern Indiana Railroad. That route, which passed through the southern tier of Michigan counties, had been completed from Detroit to Chicago two years before. Great sums of currency were being shipped by railroad express mail from the east to Chicago, the hub of the midwestern banking system. Trains were being deliberately wrecked at great loss of life and in the confusion following the tragedy the mails were being robbed.

Pinkerton accepted the assignment with the understanding that only Guthrie and his chief clerk should be aware of his findings. Because only west-bound trains carrying large sums were being attacked, he suspected someone within the post office was leaking information to the robbers.

The detective "spread out his tentacles in all directions" and, to facilitate his investigation, he rented a hotel room in Adrian, the headquarters of the chief officers of the Michigan Southern and Northern Indiana Railroad. There Pinkerton introduced himself to Joseph H. Moore, the general superintendent of the railroad, and to Albert M. Baker, chief counsel. From them he learned a startling fact - they had already employed another detective.

Moore told him a man named Augustus Stuart had written the railroad on March 27, 1854, offering his services. He claimed to have been approached by a "gang of rascals" who wanted him to participate in the wrecking and robbery of the trains. Stuart had refused and "on condition that he be given a liberal reward" offered to work with the railroad in bringing about the villains' arrest. As Pinkerton scanned Stuart's letter, he "smelled a rat." Not only did Stuart seem to know too much but he was "too wide awake to his own interests for an honest man."

Keeping his suspicions to himself for the time being, Pinkerton asked the railroad officials what they knew about Stuart. They told him he was of Scottish origin and he occasionally added "M.D." to his signature, which he also sometimes signed as Augustus Stuart Byron. Furthermore he claimed to be the natural son of Lord Byron, the great British poet. Stuart worked as a typesetter on the *Michigan Expositor* published in Adrian and "was a person of irregular habits, given to night wanderings." Pinkerton decided then and there to assign one of his detectives to work up a dossier on the mysterious young Scot.

Allan Pinkerton, America's original private eye.

The plot thickened as the detective questioned the engineers and firemen who had been on some of the wrecked trains. The *modus operandi* had varied at each crash site. Once a switch had been reversed and the train run into a gravel pit. At other times the spikes had been pulled and the rail moved slightly or a length of rail removed entirely.

Two factors remained constant, however. Only night trains heading west and carrying heavy through mails were involved and the footprints of no more than two persons were discovered at the site of the wrecks. Furthermore, one set of prints was always most prominent. They were made by boots of an English pattern with double rows of round-headed nails along the top and down the sides and heels and a heart-shaped design in the center. Pinkerton himself found and sketched a set of the prints at one of the wreck sites.

A few days later, he received an intelligence report concerning Stuart from the detective he had assigned to the case. Born in Edinburgh, Scotland, on May 24, 1817, Stuart had enlisted in the British navy as assistant surgeon at Woolwich Naval Hospital at the age of 18. During the next decade he bounced around the world to Canada, China, Holland, and England. He served as a dragoon in the U.S. Army during the Mexican War.

The year 1852 found him in Detroit, working as a printer for the *Free Press*. The following year, Stuart traveled out west with another profligate young Scot who claimed to be the son of Rear Admiral Charles Napier, commander of the British Baltic Naval Squadron. Having squandered all their money in the west, the two were returning east when the Michigan Southern and Northern Indiana Railroad train they were on collided with a Michigan Central train near Chicago. Several passengers were killed and the mails of both trains were robbed of $14,000. The thieves disappeared without a trace. But shortly thereafter Stuart and Napier began spending lavish sums in the best Chicago gaming houses.

Pinkerton instinctively felt he had his man, but thus far he had only circumstantial evidence. He needed to prove his guilt in court beyond a shadow of a doubt. The incriminating bootprints, which he suspected belonged to Stuart, seemed the most likely device to "bring this man's crime home to him."

The great detective, whose trademark featured an open eye with the motto "we never sleep," began setting his snares. First he directed the railroad officials to privately circulate an order to all employees that in the event of another wreck they were to thoroughly examine all footprints nearby before they were obliterated by curious spectators. Then he made arrangements to have a look at this other "detective."

Accordingly, a meeting was arranged in Baker's office. When Stuart arrived Pinkerton slipped into an adjoining room. As Stuart sat with his back to the door, which was slightly ajar, Pinkerton listened in on the conversation. Stuart remarked that two men, named Dean and Napier, were intending to cause another train wreck that very night, but he knew not where they would place the obstruction. Did they want him to accompany them? "I had better consult Mr. Moore first," answered Baker.

When Stuart left, Pinkerton trailed him. He made a detour around a block then passed Stuart so as to get a good look at him. He found him to be a man of average height, rather stout, with long dark hair and large bulging black eyes. Those eyes, he observed, "had a keen, restless, penetrating appearance." Stuart, who had never seen Pinkerton, paid no attention to him as he was being scrutinized.

Pinkerton returned to the office and advised Baker to tell Stuart only to follow the train wreckers. Without informing the officials, who still believed their detective to be legitimate, Pinkerton resolved to shadow him that night.

It was about nine p.m. when Stuart left Adrian. Although the night was pitch black, Pinkerton was able to follow the sound of his squeaky boots. Stuart met someone on the tracks, and they conversed in low tones. Pinkerton listened from behind a nearby fence but could not distinguish what they were saying. When the men moved on, Pinkerton lost them in the night.

He felt certain that they had already or would soon place an obstruction on the track. A train was due through shortly. If he followed Stuart, the train might pass him before he could alert the engineer and be wrecked. He could see the lights of the Adrian depot twinkling in the distance. Pinkerton hopped the fence and raced down the track toward Adrian. When he reached the station, he breathlessly blurted out the situation, urging the station master to dispatch a hand car to locate the obstruction. Then Pinkerton returned to his hiding place behind the fence.

About 20 minutes later, Stuart returned. Pinkerton followed him to a nearby cemetery and watched from behind a tombstone. Suddenly they heard the shrill whistle of the locomotive. Both men waited breathlessly - one for the sound of the inevitable crash, the other in hopes that the obstruction had been discovered in time. Fortunately, the men in the hand car had found and removed a railroad tie that had been placed on the track and the train passed safely. Stuart climbed down from his vantage point atop a tombstone and dejectedly walked back to town, where he entered a saloon and ordered a tumbler of whiskey.

Several weeks passed. Pinkerton was attending to business in Chicago when he received a telegram from Baker informing him that a train had been wrecked about three-quarters of a mile east of Adrian. The engineer had been killed. A rail placed across the track had caused the

Augustus Stuart in the Adrian cemetery anxiously awaits the train crash.

accident. Pinkerton took the next train for Adrian, where he found his instructions had been followed to the letter. The crash site had been cordoned off and guarded.

The detective soon found "the story of a great crime told in picture symbols upon the earth's surface." There were the marks of the rail being jockeyed into position and the footprints of one person as he moved back and forth across the track - footprints bearing the tell-tale heart-shaped design. The only question remaining to be solved was the ownership of the boots.

Pinkerton spent the following two weeks tramping Adrian's dusty streets, eyes downward, anxiously scanning the ground for those boot tracks. Then one afternoon following a violent thunderstorm, he found them. After he had calmed his beating heart, he followed the tracks to Baker's garden gate. He swung open the gate and saw they led straight up the sandy path to the door and back again.

Inside, Baker informed Pinkerton that Stuart had just been there and left. "What kind of boots did he have on?" questioned the detective. "Well, he usually wore fine boots, but today he had on a pair of heavy, coarse boots, with his pants tucked inside," Baker answered. Pinkerton led Baker outside and, pointing out the evidence, convinced him that Stuart had been "playing the double character of villain and detective."

Still not fully satisfied that the case against Stuart would prove foolproof in court, Pinkerton made up his mind to secure the ultimate evidence, a confession. The detective devised a clever scheme, workable in those times, but unlikely to meet with success under the current laws of evidence, arrest procedures, and treatment of the accused.

He decided his plan would work best if he arrested Stuart in Chicago. But first he made arrangements with the Chicago marshall, Darius Knight, to place Stuart in a cell with a man of Pinkerton's choice. For that purpose he hired a detective named John Black, who would masquerade as a thief known as Grover. Immediately prior to Stuart's arrest, the Chicago authorities would lock Grover up. Pinkerton hoped Stuart would discuss his nefarious activities with a fellow criminal and cell mate.

With that web in readiness, Pinkerton asked Baker to send Stuart to Chicago on detective business. The following morning Pinkerton watched Stuart's trunk, with the incriminating boots strapped on the outside, loaded on an "omnibus" for transport to the train station. Stuart checked his trunk and boarded the train for Chicago. After the last "all aboard," Pinkerton swung onto the train as well.

The train stopped at White Pigeon for a 20-minute lunch break. While Stuart and the other passengers wolfed down their meal as fast as they could at a local eatery, as was the custom of travelers of that era, Pinkerton made his way to the baggage car and filched Stuart's boots. Pinkerton had the further satisfaction of hearing Stuart curse long and loud the thief that swiped his boots when he picked up his trunk. He also wrote Moore in Adrian claiming damages for his loss.

The following day, Pinkerton had Black, alias Grover, locked in the cell. A few hours later, he collared Stuart, told him who he was and simply informed him he was a prisoner - no Miranda rights in those days. Minutes later Stuart was behind bars, in the same cell as Grover. Unfortunately for Grover, Stuart would hardly talk to him, considering him "a vulgar person far beneath his notice."

Three days later, Stuart demanded to see Pinkerton and to know for what charge he had been arrested. "Train robbery and murder," answered the detective. Then he proceeded to detail all the evidence he had on him, omitting the fact that he had the boots in his possession. Stuart blanched but maintained his innocence.

Six weeks passed. It was the heat of the summer. The cell was as hot as an oven and the prison fare was mis-

Pinkerton filches his suspect's boots from the Michigan Central Railroad car.

erable. To no avail, Grover continued to play his part well, that of a skilled burglar who would soon be released through lack of evidence. Stuart spoke to him rarely and then only about inconsequential matters.

Then Pinkerton stirred things up a bit. He had Moore pay a visit to Stuart. He elaborated on all the evidence they had collected, including the fact that Pinkerton had the boots that had been stolen and for which Stuart had claimed damages from the railroad. At first "struck dumb by the appalling array of evidence," Stuart soon rallied and denied the boots were his.

But the moment Moore left the cell, Stuart turned in desperation to Grover, who was to be liberated in a day or two. He begged Grover to help him, promising a big reward. Grover was more than happy to do whatever he could for his colleague in crime.

Stuart blurted out the whole story of his evil deeds. He even made a detailed sketch of the scene of the last train wreck. What he wanted from Grover was for him to provide an alibi, to place the damning boots on another man's feet. Stuart told Grover to testify that he had been invited to assist in the robbery by a man wearing those identical boots and had witnessed that unknown person place the rail across the tracks.

Grover agreed to tell the lie in court. To make sure he understood what to say, Stuart wrote out a script for him to memorize. The following day Grover was released, after "bidding Stuart a very affectionate adieu."

On August 2, Stuart wrote Baker asking him to use his influence to have the trial set in Adrian rather than Chicago, as he was anxious to reestablish his good name in that community. Pinkerton, who was only too happy to bypass the slow extradition process, readily agreed. Stuart was transferred to the Adrian lock-up, where he hired as his counsel Judge Peter Morey, who had served as attorney general of Michigan from 1837 to 1841.

Pinkerton learned that Morey intended to apply for a continuance at the forthcoming circuit court term. He "regarded that as the ordinary course of lawyers when they have no valid defense, to endeavor to clear their clients by wearing out the prosecution, and by causing the witnesses all the annoyance in their power," Pinkerton was not about to let that happen.

First he had Grover visit Stuart and tell him that he hoped the trial would be held within a few days as he was about to pull a big heist and, if it was successful, he would be leaving the country for a long time. Then to further confound Morey, he telegraphed from Chicago asking for a continuance because he had been summoned to Washington by the postmaster general.

Morey "swallowed the bait." He delivered a stirring appeal in court the next morning protesting further delay in the trial. Presiding Judge Warner Wing, who was also chief justice of the Michigan Supreme Court, found for the defense and the trial proceeded on schedule.

Meanwhile, Pinkerton had taken the train from Chicago, but not for Washington. He arrived in Adrian late that night and surreptitiously made his way to a private room. The next morning Pinkerton strolled down to the courthouse, quietly entered the courtroom, and took a seat. Prosecutor Alonzo F. Bixby had just finished his opening speech. Morey began addressing the jury, stressing Stuart's illustrious father, Lord Byron. He fully intended to prove "that the name of the father was not more spotless than that of the son."

As he concluded and turned to sit down, his eyes met Pinkerton's. Morey pulled off his glasses, wiped his eyes, and stared in disbelief. Pinkerton walked up, shook his hand, and congratulated Morey on his eloquent speech. Morey turned and exclaimed to his client: "I'm damned, Stuart, if old Pinkerton has not sold us."

But as the trial proceeded, Bixby seemed able to present

only a weak case. Morey and Stuart began to think they had a good chance of victory. Stuart's ace in the hole, Grover, had yet to make his appearance. They had grown so confident of the outcome, that, engaged in a *tete-a-tete*, neither even looked up when the prosecution called John Black to the witness stand.

"What is your name, sir?" asked Bixby.

"John Black," was the reply.

"Where do you reside?"

"In Chicago."

"In whose employ are you?"

"Allan Pinkerton's."

"What are your duties?"

"I am a detective, sir."

"Where did you become acquainted with the prisoner?"

"In Chicago jail."

At that moment, the heads of Morey and Stuart snapped up. Stuart's face "changed in a moment from vivid life to the ashy paleness of death." As Black continued his straightforward testimony, Stuart began to shiver uncontrollably.

Great trickles of sweat rolled down Morey's bald head, and he began nervously tearing his brief bit-by-bit into little pieces. When Black came to the part where he had been planted in the cell disguised as Grover the burglar, Morey leaped up, overturning his chair in the process. "We are sold, sir! I repeat it, sir, we are sold by that damned old Pinkerton," he thundered, as he bounced out of the courtroom.

To make a long story short, without leaving their seats the jury convicted Stuart of the two indictments of which he had been charged.

Judge Wing sentenced Stuart, alias Byron, alias McDonald, upon only one of the indictments - to a term of 99 years in Jackson Penitentiary, adding: "When the

Attorney Peter Morey reacts to damning evidence against his client.

prisoner has served the period prescribed by this sentence, I shall be happy, if I am spared till then, to sentence him on the remaining indictment."

Needless to say, that proved unnecessary. Stuart died behind the walls of Jackson Prison three years later. On his deathbed he confessed to Baker that it was he and Napier who had robbed the two trains that had collided near Chicago in 1853. That crime had been unpremeditated; they merely found themselves in an opportune position during the excitement following the crash.

That robbery had gone off so smoothly, that after they had squandered the $14,000 thus netted, they began deliberately wrecking and robbing other trains.

Napier managed to escape to Europe and Pinkerton never positively identified their confederate in the post office department.

Pinkerton continued his brilliant detective career until his death on July 1, 1884. He served as a Union spy during the Civil War, hunted Jesse James and his gang for years, and helped break up the Molly Maguires, who were active in the bloody labor troubles that disrupted the Pennsylvania coal fields in the 1870s. Pinkerton also authored 18 popular volumes that detailed his many triumphs over outlaws. Following his death, the detective agency he founded was perpetuated by his sons, Robert and William.

Although Pinkerton failed to articulate a moral in the case of the tell-tale bootprints, I cannot resist: If you choose a life of crime, you had better watch your step - or at least your footprints.

Michigan Crusaders Battle the "Tobacco Abomination"

A young smoker starts on the road to ruin.

The lumberjack leaned against his cant hook as he watched an old man and a teenaged boy striding along the railroad tracks near Pinconning. It was a crisp November morning in 1881. He turned his head to the side, spat a brown stream of tobacco juice, and shouted, "Young feller, you're a'fire, there!" The boy quickly pulled a pipe from his hip pocket and beat out the smouldering fire in his clothing.

The Reverend William F. Day, a Congregational minister from Saginaw who had conducted a rousing temperance meeting at a local lumber camp the evening before, witnessed that little incident. It led him to "wonder greatly" why "any one should be more alarmed to see smoke coming from a man's pocket than from his mouth."

By the time Reverend Day arrived back in Saginaw, he had composed a soul-stirring anti-tobacco tract which he promptly had printed and disseminated throughout the state. In it, Day stressed six good reasons why smokers should not "become a holocaust upon the altar of the filthy, unhealthy, and unwealthy tobacco abomination."

Reverend Day was but one of many who battled mightily against the pipe, stogie, chaw, and newfangled cigarette a century before the U.S. Surgeon General dared to brand tobacco products hazardous to your health. Michigan anti-tobacco campaigners were in the vanguard of the reform movement, and they carried their appeal far and wide.

None were more colorful than Alfred S. Livermore, the great "Temperance Advocate and Tobacco Agitator" who also hailed from Saginaw. Livermore described his "fight against a great monster evil" in an autobiographical volume published in 1890. Born in White Lake in Oakland County, he moved with his family to the Saginaw Valley in the late 1840s. When his mother became an invalid, Livermore dropped out of school at the age of 11 to work in a Saginaw shingle mill. In February, 1865, the 17-year-old enlisted in the Seventh Michigan Cavalry, part of George Armstrong Custer's famous Michigan Brigade.

The Civil War ended for most soldiers soon after Lee's surrender at Appomattox on April 9, 1865, but not for the men of the Michigan Brigade. To their chagrin, they were ordered out west to fight Indians for another six months and then discharged to find their own way home. In his autobiography, Livermore warmed himself up with a discussion of that grievance and then moved on to his grapples with the "monster evil."

Following the war, he had opened up a meat market and general store in East Saginaw. In 1889, two seven-year-old boys entered the store and asked to buy cigarettes. Livermore told them "the one who sells you cigarettes ought to be hung by the heels until he would promise never to sell another." That incident opened the shopkeeper's eyes to "the satanic monarch of waste and wrong." He arose from bed in the middle of the next night and burned his entire large stock of tobacco.

Although many steady customers switched stores as a result, he knew he was doing the right thing. A few loyal customers, particularly ladies, buttressed his decision. A Mrs. Shaw, for example, whose unfortunate husband had been eaten by cannibals in the South Seas six years before, backed him to the hilt. Little did she know but that, had her lamented spouse been a smoker, he might have been spared his gruesome fate. As Livermore later learned, no self-respecting cannibal would touch human flesh saturated with the vile taste of tobacco.

Not content with ruining his trade, Livermore turned activist. Armed with horrifying statistics, he went on the lecture circuit, visiting Sunday schools throughout the region. Children listened in open-mouthed attention as Livermore told them about the cannibals dread of tobacco flavored flesh. He thundered that in Chicago "five to seven boys die daily from excessive use of tobacco." Things were nearly as bad in the Wolverine state. Some 200 Michigan doctors cited cases in which boys were "being dwarfed, made insane, killed, or rendered incapable of speech" as a result of the noxious weed. Professors from the University of Michigan, Alma College, and Hillsdale College testified that "otherwise bright students were being made dull and stupid by the use of the cigarette."

If such statistics failed to convince the children, Livermores graphic examples should have. There was the case of the colored messenger boy, for example, who died suddenly in New York City. Eleven curious physicians gathered for the autopsy, and when the surgeon's knife entered the heart a strong odor of tobacco filled the room. He had died of "tobacco heart."

There were the Chicago stub pickers, who eked out an existence by picking up butts from the gutter, drying them out, and selling them to the factories to be made over into cigarettes. How could the children know but what they might smoke a "gutter-picked product," previously held between disease-saturated lips?

Cigarettes appealed largely to children and other novice smokers, including an occasional daring woman, during Livermore's era. Real men smoked cigars. President John Quincy Adams, a connoisseur of Havana cigars, had first brought respectability to the puffing of the large brown rolls. So many Bostonians followed his example that city fathers passed a law restricting cigar smokers to a certain section of Boston Commons.

Following the Civil War, popular president and war hero Ulysses S. Grant inspired a national rage for stogies. His death in 1885 of throat cancer failed to stem the tide. Bareknuckle pugilist John L. Sullivan also championed the cigar. His opinion, however, lost some of its clout when "Gentlemen Jim" Corbett, a cigarette fancier, knocked him out in 1892.

But in 1890, "eatin' tobacco" comprised nearly half of all tobacco manufactured in the United States, close to three pounds of plug, twist, or fine cut for every man,

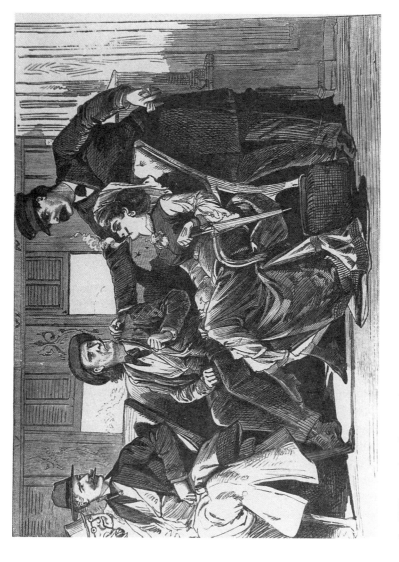

An 1877 engraving of a man about to be bounced from a railroad smoking car for allowing his wife to join him.

111

woman, and child. Among the more popular brands were Hiawatha plug and Peerless chew, manufactured at Daniel Scotten's mammoth Hiawatha Tobacco Works in Detroit.

Chewing tobacco, the preferred product of the frontier, thrived in wide open spaces where a man could let go with a stream of brown juice when and where he pleased. Not that chewing was not a feature of urban society. Photographs of the hallowed halls of Congress taken during the gilded age depict shining brass spittoons beside each member's desk. The bartender, restauranteur, or storekeeper who failed to place several cuspidors within easy reach of the public did so at the peril of his floor, rugs, and furnishings.

Livermore cited several incidents he had witnessed of the disgusting habit. When a woman passenger asked a question of a street car conductor, he was unable to answer until he had expectorated, thereby spattering her dress. Another gentleman, while visiting his pastor, emptied his mouthful into the wood box, which was subsequently encountered by the lady of the house when filling the stove.

In addition to its obviously repulsive side effects, Livermore identified tobacco use as the gateway to worse moral depravity. "Tobacco is the Devil's agent in destroying young men," he assured his audiences. Five hundred out of the 600 inmates in the Auburn, New York, state prison admitted tobacco had been the first steps in their downward course of life. Livermore traced a definite relationship between tobacco and alcohol. The boy who tried smoking would surely wind up in the grog shop. What's more, smoking produced a continual thirst for some kind of stimulating drink. Livermore himself had employed a young woman as a maid who secretly smoked in her room. She proved to be "one of the worst," if you understand his meaning.

Livermore claimed to have visited almost every city and town in the state lecturing against tobacco. He devised an anti-tobacco badge in the form of a star inscribed with the words "No Tobacco Here." Silver-plated badges sold for ten cents, gold-plated for 25 cents. He thought his badges perfect for ladies who, when asked by gentlemen, "Is smoking offensive?" might silently point to their gleaming stars.

Livermore's badge campaign was not the first of its kind. In 1876, Dr. Henry A. Reynolds stormed through Michigan on a temperance crusade that resulted in the formation of numerous red-ribbon reform clubs. Members who had signed the pledge against alcohol pinned red ribbons on their chest. "Better a red ribbon than a red nose," they told scoffers. Reynold's success spurred R.W. Boyd of Adrian to establish a Juvenile Reform Club. Boyd convinced 1,400 of Lenawee County's young boys to sign a double pledge - against alcohol as well as tobacco. They got a blue ribbon for the latter promise. In 1877, a blue ribbon army 500 strong marched to the beat of the drum down Adrian's streets to a gala reception sponsored by proud parents.

Michigan's many rhymers also waxed poetic over the tobacco abomination. Kalamazoo's most prolific poet, Joseph Bert Smiley, hawked his verse from door to door. His first volume, published in 1886, contained "Tobacco":

> What power can sanction or can bless
> That dirty, filthy cursedness?
> What demon, for a fiendish joke,
> First taught mankind to chew and smoke?

Mary T. Lathrop of Marshall, who served with distinction as president of the Michigan Women's Christian Temperance Union for 14 years, advised girls to shun the tobacco user. Her "Girls, Take Care," written in 1858, warned:

> Mark well that young man who,
> on Sabbath, would dare
> To stroll through the streets as he puffs

his cigar.

Julia Moore, the "Sweet Singer of Michigan" from rural Kent County, specialized in funeral odes. Her ballad "John Robinson" recounted the tragic story of a youth who traveled for his health to California. Alas, his sickness worsened and short on funds, he made the mistake of trying to make it home in a smoking car:

> For he was sick, and very bad -
>> Poor boy, he thought, no doubt,
> If he came home in a smoking car
> His money would hold out.
> He started to come back alone -
>> He came one-third of the way -
> One evening in the car alone
> His spirit fled away!

The tobacco fumes had done him in. The sweet singer suggested her ballad be sung to the tune of the popular temperance air, "The Drunkard."

Dr. John Harvey Kellogg of Battle Creek included in his *Sunbeams of Health and Temperance*, a compilation for youth published in 1887, the dreadful fable of "Tobacco Metamorphosis":

> When Johnny Smith was twelve years old,
>> His downward course began;
> "I guess," said he, "I"ll learn to smoke,
>> Like every other man."
> He bought himself a big cigar,
>> And down the street he went
> To puff away in filthy smoke
>> The money that he'd spent.

Within a week poor Johnny had been transformed into a chimney! The hardhearted poet then dealt him a fate worse than death:

> And now upon a roof-tree perched,
>> He moves not hand nor foot;
> His arms are cased in mortar,

The sad effects of "Tobacco Metamorphosis."

And his throat is choked with soot.

As the nineteenth century wore on, more physicians rallied to the anti-tobacco cause. Some progressive members of the medical community had, in fact, long linked tobacco with cancer. *The Medical Times and Gazette* of October 6, 1860, for example, recorded "the excision of 127 cancers from the lips, and nearly every one of the patients a smoker."

But it was Dr. Kellogg, superintendent of the Seventh Day Adventist-inspired Battle Creek Sanitarium and a tireless health reformer, who plied his pen most mightily against "the devil's favorite instruments for converting boys who might become respectable citizens and useful men, into loafers, vagabonds, drunkards, and criminals of every description." He later amplified the sentiments in "Tobacco Metamorphosis" to produce an entire volume entitled *Tobaccoism, or How Tobacco Kills.* His many kindred publications circulated throughout the country in the hundreds of thousands.

Kellogg specialized in digestive disorders, advocating hydrotherapy, daily enemas, and cold showers. He also promoted his own health foods, such as granola, peanut butter, and corn flakes. In his popular treatise on dispepsia, as indigestion was then termed, published in 1879, Kellogg wrote that "both smoking and chewing weaken and debilitate the digestive system." Some of his weight-conscious countrymen apparently gratified their oral craving by smoking instead of eating. Kellogg warned "those who succeed in keeping down fat by the use of tobacco may depend upon it that they are doing so only at the ruinous expense of their digestive organs, and may look forward with certainty to the breaking down of their own nervous systems."

Kellogg also became an early advocate of eugenics. He was convinced that tobacco users passed on to their offspring the pernicious effects of nicotine. The children of smokers and chewers, he assured his readers in 1891, "entered upon life with a weakly vital organism, with a system predisposed to disease and destined to premature decay."

Daniel Putnam, chaplain at the Michigan Insane Asylum in Kalamazoo, fully concurred with Kellogg. "By the laws of heredity," he wrote in 1885, "the effects of the habitual use of tobacco go beyond the immediate victim and the present generation, and entail a load of ills and a possible burden of woes upon posterity." Based on his 25 years of observation in the asylum, Putnam also believed tobacco use the indirect cause of much mental illness.

Kellogg, Livermore, and other anti-tobacco crusaders early championed the rights of non-smokers. Livermore thought it a "social sin" that it was impossible to "walk the public streets, or get into a crowd, and not be half strangled with tobacco smoke, or incur the risk of being fouled with tobacco juice." Those discourteous enough to eat onions before going into crowded assemblies were nothing compared to the gentlemen who "carelessly puff the smoke into anyone's face with out the least thought of apology." Kellogg asserted that non-smokers had "an undoubted right to free, fresh air as they walk the streets." "What term," he asked, "are we to apply to the act of poisoning - for tobacco smoke is a poison - the air for them to breathe."

Charles W. Post, who had imbibed Kellogg's philosophy during a two-month stay at the Sanitarium in 1891, soon established a competing health spa in Battle Creek which he named La Vita Inn. He published *I Am Well*, a mystical health manual, in 1894 and later that year tested his cereal coffee substitute, Postum, on the public's taste buds.

Quite naturally, Post devoted most of his rhetoric to the evils of coffee but he also decried tobacco as "one of the most insidious enemies of the human frame." "It's special mission," he determined, was "to tear down and neutralize all efforts of nature toward a sturdy and healthful

117

A youthful Dr. John Harvey Kellogg, anti-tobacco campaigner from Battle Creek.

manifestation in the body." It was far better, he later assured his countrymen, to relieve their "brain fag" with Postum, Grape Nuts, Post Toasties, or any of the other products from which he forged his fortune.

Battle Creek, it seems, became a hotbed of the anti -tobacco movement. Ransom Sabin, another local physician, wrote that tobacco "makes men nervous, irritable, and despondent." His 480-page guide to health, wealth, and happiness, *The Home Treasury*, published in 1890, carried the stirring appeal, "Let Tobacco Alone, Boys."

Dr. S.E. Morrill, Kalamazoo's lady medical electrician, joined her Battle Creek colleagues in their fight against tobacco in 1882. "Men die every day from paralysis of the muscles of the heart caused by tobacco," she wrote, "but because the post mortem does not reveal tobacco in the form of a leaf, doctors look wise and say, 'Died of heart disease'." After they had renounced the habit, she advised sufferers to visit her establishment for a dose of electricity which she was convinced would drain the poison from their bodies.

Another citizen of the "Celery City," Guy H. Lockwood, colorful author of *How to Live 100 Years*, took up the cause during the early years of the 20th century. Tobacco, he maintained, used up the body's "surplus energy" necessary for attaining longevity. Smokers were blowing dozens of years of their life "into soothing rings of tobacco smoke."

By Lockwood's era, fashions in tobacco use were "a -changing." Spittoons became about as scarce as cigar store Indians as the once omnipresent quid bulged the jaws of few people other than backwoodsmen and baseball players. Pipes became the domain of college professors and other literary types.

Cigars were increasingly relegated to smoke-filled rooms filled with politicians. By 1922, the little paper -covered tube of tobacco known as the cigarette was king.

Convenient, easy to smoke, and easy to stub out, cigarettes fit the helter skelter pace of a nation on the move. Beginning with the devil-may-care flappers of the roaring '20s, women too joined in the national mania for cigarettes. Rudolph Valentino and Clara Bow, Humphrey Bogart and Bette Davis made cigarettes glamorous as well.

Livermore's fight against the great monster evil slipped into oblivion. Few, other than stalwart Seventh Day Adventists, remembered Kellogg's teachings. America forgot the lessons preached by Michigan's anti-tobacco pioneers - that tobacco use causes cancer and affects the health of the unborn, that non-smokers have the right to breathe unpolluted air.

The Surgeon General's aggressive actions have spurred a recent anti-tobacco mood in this country. But then, publication of *A Counterblaste to Tobacco* by King James I in 1604, in which he decreed smoking to be "loathesome to the eye, hateful to the nose, harmful to the brain, and dangerous to the lungs" produced a similar reaction, albeit temporary. In other words, if the past holds any lessons for the present, then tobacco's future looks pretty good.

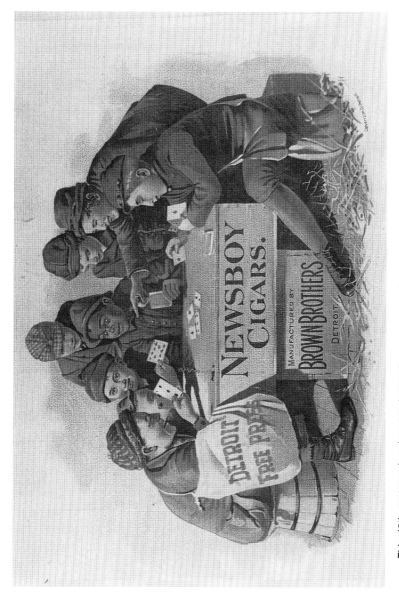

This 19th century cigar box top featured young newsboy's smoking.

Edward Israel, Michigan's Arctic Martyr

Interior of the hut at Camp Clay during cooking time.

Sgt. David Brainard staggered through the world of white, up the hill from the frozen seashore. He had enjoyed a successful day of netting and he carried his catch in two buckets. One held a mass of seaweed and the other thousands of little crustaceans about the size of a grain of wheat. Actually a type of sea lice, the American Arctic explorers who had been marooned in the far north for nearly three years preferred to call them shrimp.

It was May 6, 1884, and seven of the original party of 25 had already perished of starvation. With the exception of a few ounces of carefully hoarded scraps of meat and crumbs of bread, some sealskin thongs and leather boot soles, the sea lice and kelp Brainard carried would be the sole rations that day for the 18 servicemen left alive.

Brainard, one of the few still strong enough to walk on his own, neared the strange-looking hut the men called home. Its lower walls, made of chunks and chips of stone, were two feet thick and enclosed an area 25-feet by 18-feet.

Upon the three-foot-high stone walls the men had stretched a canvas sail over a framework of boat oars. On top of that lay a whaleboat. The entire structure was well chinked with blocks of snow to help keep out the fierce winds that sometimes lowered the wind chill to 100 degrees below zero, and colder.

Brainard pushed aside the sailcloth flap that served as a door and crawled into the hut. For a minute or so he could see nothing in the dark, smokey interior. Despite the fact that it was but a few degrees warmer inside the hut, the smell of unwashed bodies, excrement, and the breath of dying men was stifling.

The hollow-eyed men who greeted Brainard in weak voices lay huddled two and three together in sleeping bags, feet toward the center of the aisle. One poor devil had lost his feet and most of his fingers to frostbite, but still his will to live remained strong. Propped up in a sleeping bag he shared with the commander of the expedition, Lt.

Adolphus Washington Greely, sat Sgt. Edward Israel of Kalamazoo.

Israel was writing a letter, his last he suspected, to his beloved mother, Tillie, in Kalamazoo. His pencil moved slowly , painstakingly, across the sheet:

Dearest Mother,

Although our condition is not altogether desperate as yet, I take this opportunity of addressing a farewell note to you, still hoping that I may destroy it in the near future. It will not be necessary for me to detail the history of the expedition, our work, or the retreat of last fall. Will only say that the time spent at Ft. Conger was very pleasant and profitable one to me, and as you so well know, all happiness is relative. Our winter experience here was not nearly so terrible an ordeal as it must appear to you. Seven of our party have already succumbed; we have on hand about 12 days very short rations which we supplement with shrimps and seaweed. Our hunters have been so very unsuccessful this season, that the chances appear altogether against our pulling through as a party. Therefore this short note. I don't know how much longer I shall be able to write. In case I perish here, don't take my loss too seriously. My death will be an easy one and I shall make arrangements to have a companion of mine visit you if any of us should return

Please do forgive me for all the sorrow and worry I may have caused you in the past. If I had returned you would have found me a changed man.

Still hoping that things may take a more favorable turn, than I anticipate, believe me.

Yours,
Edward Israel

Israel sank back, exhausted from the effort of writing the letter. He let his mind wander back to his hometown and to the events that had placed him in such a God forsaken situation.

Mannes Magnus Israel, Edward's father had emigrated from Pyrmont, Germany, to Kalamazoo in 1844. The first Jewish citizen to reside in the village, he established a prosperous dry goods business at a shop located at the corner of Michigan Avenue and Rose Street. Edward, born in Kalamazoo on July 1, 1859, was one of five children sired by the elder Israel. His father, however, died when Israel was a small child. An older brother, Joseph, assisted Tillie Israel in running the dry goods store.

Tillie devoted herself to the care of the children and Edward received a fine early education from her. Upon entering the Kalamazoo public school system, "his progress was rapid and sure." Israel remained in Kalamazoo until 1878 when he enrolled in the University of Michigan. There he studied mathematics, astronomy and surveying, gaining a reputation as "one of the ablest of his classes."

Israel was in his senior year during the spring of 1881 when he learned of an opportunity to participate in a scientific expedition to the Arctic. Greely had sent letters to professors at several leading universities, seeking the services of a young man trained in astronomy and mathematics to accompany the U.S. government sponsored expedition he was fitting up. Greely's goal was to set up a post on Lady Franklin Bay, Ellesmere Island, a few miles west of the coast of Greenland and 500 miles south of the North Pole. That base camp, from which meteorological, magnetic, and other scientific data would be collected, was to be the farthest north of a ring of 12 such stations maintained by various nations participating in the first International Polar Year.

Three days after Greely had sent out his inquiry, Professor Mark W. Harrington of the Astronomical Observatory at Ann Arbor responded:

Members of the Greely Arctic Expedition: second from left seated, David Brainard, fourth, Adolphus Greely, sixth, Edward Israel.

Dear Sir:

In reply to your favor of the 1st [April] I would nominate Mr. Edward Israel for the position refered to. He is an unusually bright man, a member of the senior class; has strong mathematic and scientific tastes and desires to make the pursuit of astronomy a specialty. He has already had sufficient practice with the sextant and transit to successfully undertake determination of time, latitude and longitude and has sufficient mechanical aptitude to readily pick up any class of observation which he might be required to make. I think he would do very creditable work and I should be glad to see him appointed. He has already signified his willingness to go if appointed...

Following receipt of a medical examination testifying to Israel's ability to withstand the rigors of Arctic service, Greely accepted Harrington's recommendation. The University of Michigan obligingly granted Israel his diploma prior to the normal graduation time. Anxious to train his party and be off as soon as possible, Greely allowed Israel only a quick return to Kalamazoo. There the 21-year-old requested and received his mother's reluctant permission to go on the expedition and bid friends and family a hasty farewell.

Israel left Kalamazoo on April 28, 1881, arriving in Washington three days later. There he was sworn into the U.S. Army Signal Corps and promoted to the rank of sergeant at a salary of $100 per month. Practically all of the other men who had volunteered for the mission were veteran soldiers, seasoned by tough frontier duty. Israel was the youngest, the only Jew, and with the exception of the expedition's surgeon, the only member with a university degree. Posing with the others for a group photograph in Washington, he was also the only man lacking a moustache or beard.

On June 9, the expedition sailed from Washington for St.

John's Newfoundland.   From there, they boarded a commercial sealing vessel for transport to their final destination, Lady Franklin Bay.

The vessel managed to get through the ice flow that normally clogged Smith Sound and the Kane Basin even in the summer, because the year had been an unusually warm one. The expedition members, however, did not realize that their ease in getting that far north had been the result of a seasonal anomaly.

The men unloaded material for building a sturdy structure that would enable them to survive in the frigid zone, plus ample supplies for a two-year stay.   They named the post Fort Conger, in honor of Michigan Senator Omar D. Conger, who had sponsored the bill that allocated $25,000 for the venture

The expedition members spent the succeeding two years in collecting valuable scientific data. Israel accomplished his important   observation duties with distinction.   From the base, Brainard and Lt. James Lockwood conducted an exploration trek that set a record for the farthest north anyone had heretofore reached. Despite the bitter cold, the many months each year that saw little or no light day, the isolation and boredom, the men were well-fed and remained in good spirits.

Ominously, the ship that was to land additional supplies during the summer of 1882 failed to get through the ice. Another long year came and went. The sun disappeared on October 14 and did not appear again until the end of February.   Then came days measured in minutes, that lengthened to hours, then steadily grew longer and longer until for 20 weeks in summer no night fell at all. But even in July, the mean temperature rose to only 37.1 degrees Fahrenheit.   In February, the coldest month, the mean temperature dropped to 40.1 below zero. For the entire two years they were at Fort Conger, a mere 7.77 inches of precipitation fell. They were surviving in an Arctic desert

Fort Conger on Lady Franklin Bay.

in which it was too cold to snow. But what snow fell never completely melted, even in summer. The men supplemented their rations at Fort Conger by hunting wild musk oxen, seals, and ducks. They celebrated holidays with festive feasts. Each man was issued an entire quart of rum on his birthday. In true camaraderie, developed through living together in such close quarters, most passed the bottle around until empty. Other entertainment included a lecture series the men put together, chess, checkers, cards, and reading and rereading the limited number of books on hand. During the third summer, many spent their leisure time eagerly scanning the horizon for first sight of the ship that was to carry them home.

By August, as the summer days began to wane, they knew they looked in vain. The prearranged plan in the event of such a calamity was for the party to retreat south down the coast of Smith Sound in small boats to a point known as Cape Sabine. There they expected to find a large cache of supplies.

On August 9,1883, the men loaded remaining supplies onto the boats and pushed off from the shelter that had allowed them to survive in relative comfort during two Arctic years. Cape Sabine lay 225 miles south, and by August 26 the men had gained sight of their goal. But that night the boats became frozen fast in the ice. For days they remained trapped, until - leaving the largest crafts behind - they pushed on. Then came weeks of dragging the supplies over ragged mountains of ice.

Meanwhile, Israel had discovered through his astronomical calculations that the northerly flow of the current was cancelling out each day's progress. Miraculously, however, the current shifted and they finally managed to reach land after 34 days adrift on the ice.

With few rations left, Greely sent an advance party to locate the supplies at Cape Sabine. The men returned with the worst possible news. The relief ship *Proteus*, had been " nipped" in the ice, its hull crushed by the irresistible force, and sent to the bottom. The crew and relief party had abandoned ship in time to save only a small amount of supplies. They had left roughly 1,000 rations at Cape Sabine before pushing south to save their own lives.

Those rations, a few hundred pounds of goods that might be salvaged from caches left by previous explorers and whatever fresh meat the hunters might be fortunate enough to kill, would have to sustain 25 men for the next nine months. The explorers made their way to Cape Sabine and constructed the hut they named Camp Clay in honor of a friend who was leading the campaign back home to mount a relief expedition.

The men discovered all of this information in scraps of newspaper that were wrapped around some lemons left by the Proteus rescue party. That was their first intelligence from the outside world in more than two years.

Greely reduced the daily food allowance to one-fifth of the normal Arctic ration. As the men grew weaker, most began spending more and more time in their sleeping bags. There was only enough splinters of wood, hanks of rope, and other bits of fuel to cook their meager rations each day, nothing to burn for heating purposes. The men's breath kept the temperature inside the hut only a little above that of the outside. With everything frozen and no fire to melt the ice, lack of drinking water also became a constant worry. Some men tried to thaw ice in their sleeping bags, others sucked chips of ice.

Game proved nearly non-existent in that bleak environment. Once during the winter, the men were lucky enough to kill a bear. Occasionally they shot at point-blank range one of the Arctic foxes that prowled around the camp. Weighing about four pounds, every part of those unlucky carnivores, from entrails to paws, was eagerly devoured.

The tiny shrimp made the difference between life and

The men of the Greely Expedition bury the first to starve to death.

death. A good day's catch ranged from two to 15 pounds. Israel computed that it took 1,300 of the miniscule sea lice to fill a four-ounce measure. Yet they contained little nourishment.

The first man died of starvation on January 17, 1884. Despite the overwhelming likelihood that a similar fate awaited them most of the party bore their ordeal stoically. Their thoughts and conversation naturally centered on food. They spent endless hours planning the feasts they would enjoy back home. Each lovingly described the favorite dish he would supply: roast turkey, pork chops, Irish stew, peaches and cream, flapjacks and molasses, clam chowder. Israel promised his mother's incomparable "hashed liver."

The pangs of hunger brought out the worst in a few of the men. Israel recorded in his diary how the surgeon, Dr. Octave Pavy, filched food from the man he was supposed to be nursing. Another desperate villain, who remained strong and healthy, was detected robbing the food stores. After repeated warnings, Greely later ordered him shot. Worse yet, some of their number, unbeknownst to the others, were hacking chunks of flesh off those who had died . The cannibal or cannibals were never positively identified.

Such was the pitiful state that the band of explorers had been reduced to by May 6 when Israel wrote his last letter. Although Greely had listed him, on April 18, as being "in a very bad way," the Michigan youth clung tenaciously to life. One by one, the hardy frontier soldiers breathed their last, but still Israel lived on.

On May 23, those who were able evacuated the hut because the heavy layer of ice, which had formed on the canvas ceiling from their breath, was melting and saturating them. They moved to a tent further up the hill. Israel was able to walk only halfway; someone stronger hauled him the rest of the distance.

Three days later, unable to sit up or feed himself, his mind rambled as "he talked much of his home and younger days." About three a.m. on May 27, Israel "died very easily." Brainard scrawled a farewell tribute in his pocket diary:

"Everyone was his friend. He had no enemies. His frankness, his honesty, and his noble generosity of nature had won the hearts of all his companions. His unswerving integrity during these months of agony has been a shining example; and although his sacrifices were lost to a few, still the effect has produced good fruit. For lack of strength we could not bury him today."

When finally the men could drag him to a nearby spot they had named Cemetery Ridge and shovel a few inches of gravel over his body, Greely delivered the burial service. He chose his text from the Old Testament out of respect to Israel's religion.

Three more weeks of suffering passed. Dr. Pavy had died; Pvt. Henry, the thief, had been shot; all were gone but seven. They lay inside the half-collapsed tent, listening to the moanings of a gale-force wind, waiting for their end to come as well. Suddenly they heard the sound of running feet. A Navy rescue mission headed by Commander Winfield Scott Schley, who would later distinguish himself during the Spanish-American War, had broken through the pack ice.

Soon the seven survivors were chewing biscuits and pemmican, and bundled in warm blankets, conveyed to the relief vessel, the *Bear*. Pitifully, Cpl. Joseph Elison, who had lost his feet and hands to frostbite, died on the return voyage. But Greely, Brainard, and four others lived to tell the world of their terrible ordeal. Greely and Brainard remained in the army and both rose to the rank of general. Greely died in 1935 at the age of 91, Brainard in 1946, age 89.

Israel's sealed casket arrived in Kalamazoo on August 11, 1884. A crowd of 3,000 mourners waited at the Michigan Central depot to pay their last respects to the "worthy

The rescue; Commander Windfield Scott Schley in center.

brave, and noble-hearted son of Kalamazoo."   Downtown stores closed in respect as a procession of city police and firemen, Mayor Allen Potter and other city officials, and representatives of fraternal orders escorted the horse-drawn hearse from the depot, up Burdick Street along Michigan Avenue to the Israel residence in the 500 block of West Michigan.   There the closed casket lay in state while the public paid its honors.

Israel was buried in the Jewish section of Mountain Home Cemetery.   In 1972, a state historical marker was erected nearby his grave, perpetuating the memory of the Kalamazoo youth who gave his life in the name of science.

Mediums, Mesmerists & Mystic Medics: Spiritualism in Battle Creek

The religion founded by two teenaged sisters in 1848 featured bizarre symbolism.

Before Battle Creek earned fame as a mecca for jaded and dyspeptic invalids seeking cures at Dr. John Harvey Kellogg's world-famous Sanitarium, well before America crunched its breakfast out of boxes marketed from "The Cereal City," and long before thousands convened there to crane their necks at a sky filled with rainbow-hued balloons, the community had established a reputation as a haven for followers of a strange new cult - spiritualism.

During the mid-19th century, Battle Creek vied with Buffalo, New York, for title as America's spiritualist headquarters. From across the country came mediums, clairvoyants, mesmerists, mystic medics, and other occult practitioners to consult Calhoun County's deceased denizens.

Settled in the 1830s by pioneers largely from New York and the New England states, the community lay along the old Territorial Road at the confluence of the Kalamazoo River and the Battle Creek. The creek and the settlement drew their name from a drunken fight between two surveyors and two Potawatomi in 1825 during which an Indian got his skull broken and the surveyors withdrew for reinforcements. Governor Lewis Cass patched up the hard feelings, but the skirmish grew into a battle with each telling by the participants.

Calhoun County comprised a prime wheat-growing region and Battle Creek, where water power from two streams could be harnessed, proved a good site for flour and other mills. When the Michigan Central Railroad snaked out from Detroit in 1845, the future seemed secure for the little village.

By 1850, more than 1,000 people resided in nearly 200 structures scattered along Battle Creek's dusty streets. Yet, cows outnumbered horses within the village. Flour mills, woolen mills, lard oil mills, shoe factories, and the newly established Nichols and Shepard plow works turned out most of the town's products. But it wasn't train loads of wheat, wool, and plows that brought Battle Creek its first national fame. By the mid-1850s, the city had become a haven where adherents of unorthodox and sometimes bizarre creeds received sanctuary.

America of the pre-Civil War era had its share of unusual new movements. From western New York came Joseph Smith and the Mormon religion and William Miller, whose predictions of the speedy end of the world sent thousands of Millerites scurrying to hilltops to greet the Judgment Day. The voices of abolitionists thundered against slavery, vegetarians renounced meat for graham crackers, young doctors staged ether parties where their lady friends grew high on the newly discovered "pain killer," traveling phrenologists felt cranial bumps for signs of character, and P.T. Barnum made a fortune based on the adage "there's a sucker born every minute."

Battle Creek developed into a community exceptionally tolerant of many of these eccentric new beliefs, but why is something of a mystery. Perhaps the population included a heavier proportion of pioneers from the "burned-over" district of western New York which became known as the "Psychic Highway" for giving rise to a variety of strange religions. Maybe local "Underground Railroad" conductor Erastus Hussey and his Quaker brethren seeded the town's tolerance.

Following a lecture in Battle Creek in 1866, Ralph Waldo Emerson noted in his journal that the local residents "are anxious for the success of radical politics." Pioneer historian Anson Van Buren wrote that the city had "ever been a place where 'isms' readily take root and flourish." For whatever reason, there is no denying that diverse and peculiar ideologies found a home in Battle Creek.

A band of Quakers, outspoken anti-slavery activists, settled in Battle Creek in the 1830s. Sometime during the next decade, followers of Emanuel Swedenborg organized a New Jerusalem church. Swedenborgians believed their master had accomplished direct communication with the spiritual world. Battle Creek, according to Van Buren, was the only town in the country to host both a Swedenborgian and Quaker church. The Universalists, considered daring non-conformists by mid-19th century standards, also established a church on Jefferson Street. Spiritualism, perhaps the most eccentric creed to come out of the period, soon gained a firm footing in Battle Creek which became "a sort of spiritualistic headquarters."

The belief that spirits survive physical death and can influence the living runs as a common thread through many primitive religions. The history of christianity is punctuated with episodes of witch mania, poltergeists, and demonic possession. But "events" in a small frame house located in the village of Hydesville, New York, in 1848 gave rise to a mass religious movement known as modern American spiritualism.

Mysterious footsteps and rappings, unexplained movement of objects, unseen touches, and other strange occurrences had troubled the occupants of the structure - the Fox family - for some months after taking up residence in the old cottage. Margaretta and Catherine, teen-aged sisters, experimented and discovered they could communicate with the invisible noisemaker who rapped out answers to their questions. The "spirit" related that he had been a 31-year-old peddler who was murdered in the house for his money some five years before. When neighbors gathered to witness the phenomenon, he knocked for them as well. The Fox sisters began demonstrating their skills as mediums before growing audiences in nearby Rochester. Soon "The Rochester Rappers" inspired others to take up the new religion that proved "there is no death."

Spiritualists claimed that "city streets are thronged with an unseen people who flit about us, jostle us in thick crowds, and in our silent halls, our secret chambers, and our busiest haunts; their piercing eyes, invisible to us, are scanning all our ways." Through the "spiritual telegraph"

The "Rochester Rappers," Catherine and Margaretta Fox.

141

of sensitive mediums such as the Fox sisters, spirits eagerly shared their secrets with the living. As a spiritualistic epidemic swept the country and scores of converts wrote ghostly tracts, many others discovered that they, like the Foxes, had powers of occult communication. Soon ouija boards, spirit slate writing, table tippings, and seances enriched American popular culture.

Spiritualist lecturers who toured Battle Creek in the early 1850s evidently first struck a responsive chord among members of the Quaker community. Warren Chase, for example, a former Fourier socialist and prominent spiritualist author and promoter known as "The Lone One," delivered a course of lectures at the Quaker meeting house in 1853. He was so well received that he returned two years later to settle in the newly platted Quaker community of Harmonia, located six miles west of Battle Creek. The name Harmonia comes directly from the spiritualist doctrines widely promulgated by Andrew Jackson Davis, an apostle of the cult known as "The Poughkeepsie Seer." Also at Harmonia during the 1850s, Quakers Reynolds Cornell and his son Hiram ran a spiritualist-oriented academy.

In 1857, Sojourner Truth, the famous abolitionist and women's rights and temperance advocate, purchased a lot in Harmonia. Sojourner was apparently not a spiritualist, but was attracted to the Quakers of Harmonia because they also came from Ulster County in New York, where she had spent the first 30 years of her life as a slave. Nevertheless, most other residents of Harmonia practiced spiritualism, and by 1858 the movement had grown to such an extent that Chase could notify fellow believers that Battle Creek was "the most lively and enterprising station between Detroit and Chicago, where our cause and friends are in the ascendant."

Much of spiritualism's local success revolved around the charismatic leadership of James M. Peebles, "The Spiritual Pilgrim." Peebles, a gaunt giant of a man, dressed in black and sporting the long hair and beard of a biblical patriarch, arrived to guide the Battle Creek "rappers" in 1856. He had grown up in western New York in the 1820s and became a Universalist minister. He converted to spiritualism in 1856 after chancing to share a room in a Cleveland hotel with the celebrated touring mediums, the Davenport brothers. Ira and William Davenport, with the assistance of their spirit friend, John King, were then thrilling audiences with demonstrations of levitation while a spirit voice spoke from a suspended trumpet.

Peebles flippantly dared the brothers' spirit guides to appear and then went to bed. As related in his 1871 biography, the spirits rapped him awake in the middle of the night, rocked his bed, pummeled him around the room, and then announced: "You are appointed for a great work; gird up your loins, buckle on your sandles, grasp the sword of truth. Go forth!" A few months later, Peebles accepted the pastorship of Battle Creek's "First Free Church."

Peebles launched his new duties with enthusiasm and periodically augmented his congregation with converts. Two years later, for example, Peebles joined a traveling mesmerist in staging a demonstration of the hypnotic arts. One of the local rowdies thought he'd expose them both as charlatans and volunteered for the hypnotic experiment.

However, when the mesmerist put "young Dunn" into a "magnetic sleep" on the stage, he went into convulsions, "a species of trance peculiar to disorderly mediumship," Peebles announced. Dunn's hand moved as if he were writing. When given a pen, he scribbled a garbled message in "an unknown tongue." Peebles quickly held the manuscript before a mirror and read: "I was killed on the Great Western Railroad, near Hamilton, Canada West, two hours ago. I have a wife and two children in Buffalo. John Morgan."

Peebles garnered plenty of new believers when the following week's paper brought news of the accident and John Morgan's death. Dunn, a confirmed spiritualist as a

James M. Peebles, the "Spiritual Pilgrim."

result of his experience, served an apprenticeship under "The Spiritual Pilgrim" before launching his own lucrative career as a traveling stage medium.

Flushed with success as a result of his platform-hypnotism debut, Peebles branched into lecturing on morality and temperance and encountered spirits of another sort. He thundered to an audience in Van Buren County's Decatur: "Let no man who swears come within four feet of me; six feet who chews tobacco; ten feet who drinks whiskey."

A local judge, something of a tosspot, tottered toward the stage waving a $10 gold piece and announced that the speaker should be paid well for his eloquence. As Peebles reached out, the judge teetered back four feet and squealed, "I sometimes swear," then wavering back six feet, said, "I chew tobacco," then back ten feet, "I drink whiskey," and plunged the half eagle back in his pocket. The house roared and Peebles' performance was over for the night.

As Peebles proselytized the surrounding countryside, he encountered and befriended other mediums and spirits. A woman medium from Albion helped him contact the spirit of Chief Powhatan of colonial Virginia fame and the father of Pocahontas. Powhatan liked Peebles, whom he called "Preach." He clairvoyantly conveyed news of the western Indian wars weeks before the events hit the newspapers and in general became Peebles' special guardian spirit.

The chief set about to cure his consumptive friend "Preach," whom the doctors had given up on, through his knowledge of secret herbal remedies. Powhatan led the entranced Peebles to certain wild plants, showed him how to pound them into medicines, and even woke him throughout the night to gulp down the elixirs. Within months Peebles was a new man, eager to pass on his newly acquired medical acumen to local sufferers.

Despite Powhatan's guidance, Peebles found it difficult to scrape up a living in Battle Creek and in 1860 he wandered off to California to seek his fortune. Chase, Benjamin Todd, and other prominent local "rappers" took over the spiritualist pulpit. In 1862 Peebles returned to Battle Creek, but five years later, "hoping for a more lucrative locality for a living," he and his wife headed for New Jersey.

Peebles turned from the rostrum to the pen and began cranking out such popular spiritualist tracts as *The Christ Question Settled* and *Hell Revised, Modernized and Made More Comfortable.* Some titles reportedly sold 75,000 copies. While "his trumpet gave no uncertain sound" concerning the spirit world, Peebles also printed his and Powhatan's medical lore in *Vaccination a Curse and a Menace to Personal Liberty, Death Defeated, or the Psychic Secrets of How to Keep Young,* and his best seller, *How to Live a Century and Grow Old Gracefully.*

Although bereft of "The Spiritual Pilgrim," spiritualism in Battle Creek remained vital. Chase and other local seers were assisted in their labors by several Albion spiritualist celebrities. Dr. Slade moved to Albion from New York to specialize in spirit slate writing. Under his mediumship, messages from the "Other World" automatically appeared in chalk. Dr. Slade also enlisted the services of a faithful Indian spirit guide, Owasso, to demonstrate levitation and the transportation of lost objects from far off places to Albion.

Another Albion medium, A.B. Whiting, preferred spirit pictures as proof. While sitting for an ambrotype, small faces mysteriously appeared on the exposed plate. Upon close examination, Whiting said he recognized turbaned faces about the size of a dime, "members of a band of Persian spirits" who accompanied his special spirit, "The Old Man." Whiting also published popular spiritualist sheet-music songs including "Waiting Only Waiting and Land of the So Call Dead."

In March of 1877 speakers from across the country,

including "some 50 celebrated mediums," flocked to Battle Creek's Stewart Hall to celebrate the 29th anniversary of modern spiritualism. The special correspondent of the *Niles Democrat* reported that the city "is the stronghold of spiritualism, as it is of Adventism - the head center you might say."

The gala event opened with an invocation delivered under direct spirit influence and, as large framed portraits of Thomas Paine and Powhatan hung overhead, mediums began delivering orations in "various unknown tongues." Unfortunately, the celebrants were disappointed during the evening session when a special seance failed because "conditions were not right." Spiritualists thronged to the shores of Goguac Lake again during the summer of 1881 for the annual camp meeting of the state association.

Spiritualism remained a force to be reckoned with in 19th century Battle Creek. Of course, some dared the occult forces by laughing at the table tippings and rappings. Chief among spiritualism's antagonists were members of the Seventh Day Adventist Church.

The Adventists, an offshoot of the disappointed Millerite movement, had moved from Rochester to Battle Creek in 1855. Prophetess Ellen G. White and her husband, James White, led the church in making Battle Creek one of the midwest's largest printing centers from which flowed a torrent of fundamentalist tracts. Sister White, whose divine visions dictated Adventist policy, decreed that the spiritualists talked not to the dead but to devils. Battle Creek, the Whites decided, wasn't big enough for two religions based on direct communication with the other world, and the Adventists fought the hated spiritualists tooth and nail.

In the 1860s, Sister White learned in vision that the daring short skirt and pantaloon ensemble popularized by Amelia Bloomer should be worn by Adventist ladies for health reasons. For similar reasons, the spiritualists also

Sister Ellen G. White, Seventh Day Adventist seer.

adopted the bloomer outfit en masse. "Frequently," Sister White lamented, "strangers would ask, 'are you spiritualists'?" After suffering such comparisons for a few years, the Adventists quietly returned to normal fashions.

Adventist dogma swung more and more to health reform. Sister White's visions promoted vegetarianism, anti-tobaccoism, and the hydropathic or water-cure regimen. To further promote their health theories, the Adventists established a hydropathic institute that eventually evolved under Dr. John Harvey Kellogg into the famous Battle Creek Sanitarium. Interesting competition for the lucrative health market kept the Adventists busy. Dr. Dye from Marshall promised to restore lost manhood with his "voltaic belt" and Mrs. Ellen Overholt, a Battle Creek "electrician," shocked her patients back to fitness.

Spiritualism's relationship with quack healers attracted investigations from the traditional medical profession which cast shadows on the entire religion. Adventist theology might not topple spiritualism, but perhaps its common sense health reforms could. Yet, spiritualism continued as a belief well into the 20th century, gaining such powerful advocates as Sir Arthur Conan Doyle of Sherlock Holmes fame and Michigan novelist Stewart Edward White. But the movement weakened in Battle Creek by the end of the 19th century.

When the spiritualists held a national convention in conjunction with the Columbian Exposition in 1893, not a single delegate hailed from Battle Creek. But three years later, a new cycle of psychic excitement as well as one of the period's most colorful medical scams began with the reappearance of Peebles, "The Spiritual Pilgrim."

Peebles had led a busy life after he relinquished his ministerial duties in Battle Creek in 1867. He collaborated with J.O. Barrett, his biographer, to publish a hymn book in Boston in 1868. The following year he served briefly as United States consul to Trebinzonde, a Turkish Black Sea port. Peebles stayed on the move, traveling three times around the globe to study spiritualism and magic. These experiences, in conjunction with spiritual communication with notable deceased physicians of all ages, led him to decide "the soul and soul forces are the great healers."

Pausing to pick up a quick medical degree from a fraudulent Philadelphia diploma mill in 1876, "Dr." Peebles continued his search for more lucrative sites to conduct his ministrations. He set up psychic healing institutes in New Jersey, Texas, and California. Then in 1896, the 73-year-old, white bearded giant, resembling "King Lear tailored by Brooks Brothers," hung the shingle for the Dr. Peebles Institute at 350 Madison Street back in Battle Creek. He chose for his motto, "Health is the foundation of success" - his continued success, Peebles hoped.

Dr. J.A. Burroughs and his wife went into partnership with Peebles. Burroughs, in reality Peebles' adopted son, possessed occult powers of "determining the secret cause of chronic disease." Mrs. Burroughs, who judging from her portrait would have been more comfortable at a carnival, specialized in ladies who preferred "the counsel of their own sex in certain matters." Dr. Peebles himself handled "cases of peculiar nature in which no ordinary method of relief is efficient."

The Peebles-Burroughs method combined medical science with mediumship to focus psychic powers "with determination until the all-important question is settled." Sufferers unable to make it to Battle Creek merely sent in a description of their complaints with pre-payment and the team of mediums mailed back the diagnosis and cure. "Hundreds of patients who have been speedily cured," Peebles assured, "have never seen the doctors who treated them."

In 1910, a grand jury indicted Peebles for claiming that he had the power of Christ to cure all ills and even restore

How some mediums accomplished spirit slate writing.

life. Journalist Malcolm Bingay covered the trial in the U.S. District Court in Detroit. He recalled the sensational court proceedings in his autobiography:

"District Attorney Gordon bellowed at Peebles on the stand: 'Do you, before this jury of God-fearing men, now claim, under oath, that you have the powers of our Lord and Savior Jesus Christ to heal the sick and restore the dead to Life?'

"Peebles rose from the chair to his full height of six-feet-four and raised his fist above his head. He looked like Moses in a Cecil de Mille supercolossal. 'I do!' he cried in a rich baritone voice that reverberated through the court chambers. 'I do!!' And may God strike me dead on this spot if I am not possessed of such power! He gave it to me. Speak O God, and give this jury the proof! The proof!"

"The jury and I waited for divine action. The air was tense... Peebles stood there with his arm still high, waiting, waiting, waiting. For about a minute he stood, then relaxed. He turned to the jury in a soft purring voice and said: 'Gentlemen, you see for yourself."

After the jury convicted Peebles of practicing fraudulent medicine, he turned from his psychic scheme to a mail-order patent medicine racket - the Peebles Epilepsy Cure. Later, Pure Food and Drug Act chemist found his "brain restorative and nerve tonic" to contain no active ingredients and fined the company.

By 1915, Peebles had left Battle Creek to pursue his profession under sunny California skies. Seven years later, the flamboyant author of *How to Live a Century and Grow Old Gracefully* died just one month short of his 100th birthday.

With Peebles passed a colorful era in American popular culture. He was one of the last of the spiritualist pioneers. The final member of the Fox family who had startled the 19th century world with their occult demonstrations in 1848 died in 1902. The denouement to the Fox family annals, however, would not be revealed until two years later. A yellowed clipping from the *Rochester Democrat and Chroncile*, found inserted in an old spiritualist tract, documents a final bit of chilling evidence:

HUMAN BONES DISCOVERED

"Newark, November 12 [1904] - William H. Hyde, a well-known citizen of Newark and owner of the old spook house in which modern spiritualism originated March 31, 1848, reported a startling discovery today.   Mr. Hyde, while at the house Sunday, discovered human bones consisting of vertebrae, rib, arm and leg bones, a shoulder blade and collar bone. It seems that the north cellar wall of the old house fell in recently and as a result the bones were exposed..."

The house at Hydesville, where modern Spiritualism began in 1848.

If Only the Walls Could Talk: The Story of White Pigeon's Land Office

A modern view of the White Pigeon Land Office.

$\mathcal{A}$ squat little building - plain, unpretentious, and sturdy like the pioneers who built it - stands on West Chicago Road in the heart of White Pigeon. Those unattuned to the classic simplicity of Greek Revival architecture might label it homely . But if you look past its humble facade into its heart, you can experience one of the oldest and most historic structures still standing in southwest Michigan.

It's a miracle how it survived the vicissitudes of time. In the 19th century, a careless inhabitant might have knocked over a kerosene lamp and ended its existence. It might have burned down in the great fire of 1906 that devastated much of the southern St. Joseph County village. The tornado that ripped apart the Eddy Paper Mill in 1914 might also have sent the little building skyward like Dorothy's Kansas house in *The Wizard of Oz.*. More likely, some Philistine developer who coveted the location might have bulldozed it.

Luckily, the "might-haves" have not happened. Not only has it survived; a dedicated group of historians have restored the land office to its former glory.

The building was constructed prior to June 1, 1831. For three years following that date, it housed the United States Land Office for the Michigan Territory.

The story of how all of this came to pass begins in 1815. The War of 1812, during which plenty of American scalps swung from Indian belts and the River Raisin ran red with blood, had ended. An appreciative Congress had voted to give military veterans six million acres of bounty land in the west.

Edward Tiffin, formerly a governor of Ohio and then surveyor general, was charged with locating two million acres of good farmland in the Michigan Territory. Instead, he authored a report that described Michigan's terrain as an interminable swamp unfit for human habitation. Largely as a result of such adverse publicity, the immigrants who poured into the Old Northwest Territory bypassed Michigan for Ohio, Indiana, and Illinois.

In 1817 Tiffin, one of Ohio's premier promoters, also planted the seeds of the controversy that erupted into the "Toledo War" in 1835. He directed a survey of Michigan's southern border that awarded a seven mile wide wedge on the territory's southeastern border, known as the, "Toledo Strip" to Ohio. When the territory applied for statehood in 1833, Buckeye congressmen blocked Michigan's entrance into the union until Ohio's version of the boundary was accepted.

As late as the mid-1820s, with the exception of an occasional fur trader, few white men had ventured into Michigan's interior. Two events happened in 1825 that changed all that.

The opening of the Erie Canal allowed cheap and relatively rapid transportation through New York state to Buffalo and hence by steamer to Detroit. Secondly, Congress appropriated $10,000 for a survey to build a military road linking Detroit with Chicago.

The surveyor who started west from Detroit had good intentions of running a straight road, but he soon realized the appropriation was far too meager. A practical man, he chose an expedient that should have been obvious from the start. He ran his survey down the middle of an ancient Indian path known as the Sauk Trail because it was the route used by Black Hawk and his Sauk tribesmen for their annual pilgrimage from Illinois to Fort Malden in Canada to receive presents from the British. As a result, the Sauk Trail became the Detroit-Chicago Military Road, the primary east-west route for pioneer immigrants. It is now known as U.S. 12.

The surveyor who crossed southern Michigan found - instead of Tiffin's endless swamps - beautiful park-like oak openings interspersed with fertile prairies. When news of these discoveries filtered eastward, thousands of pioneers, primarily from New York and the New England states, began heading for "Michigania."

Pioneers streamed into Michigan in the 1830s to carve homesteads out of the wilderness.

Government land sold for $1.25 an acre, and the federal government was anxious to sell it. Once the Michigan wilderness had been surveyed into townships and sections, and put on the market, it was first-come, first-serve and the devil take the hindmost. Some even pre-empted land ahead of the surveys, but these "squatters" risked losing their claims to whoever first registered and paid for the land. The Federal Land Office for the Michigan Territory, where this transaction needed to take place, was initially located at Detroit in 1818 and moved to Monroe in 1823.

The first pioneers who ventured into southwest Michigan marveled at the pristine beauty of the lush 18,000-acre tract named White Pigeon Prairie. They had equal praise for Prairie Ronde in Kalamazoo County and the other smaller prairies that dotted the region.

The earliest arrivals quickly snapped up the choice prairie land. John Winchell and Arba Heald journeyed from Monroe in 1826 to stake out their claims, and the following year they became the first settlers on White Pigeon Prairie. Asahel Savery and Robert Clark Jr. entered tracts in 1828. Clark, who worked on the survey of the military road, like several other early surveyors used his advance knowledge to invest in choice plats.

The remainder of the prairie soon felt the bite of heavy breaking plows as pioneer farmers hawed and geed their ox teams. A little settlement sprang up at the junction of the military road and a meandering trail that ran north to Kalamazoo County. Storekeepers set up shop and entrepreneurs opened grist and saw mills.

By 1831 White Pigeon boasted a population of 600. It was a natural stopping place for the hordes of immigrants who streamed into southwest Michigan, and it seemed the logical place to relocate the federal land office. Accordingly, on June 1, 1831, the office was officially moved from Monroe to White Pigeon. Thomas Sheldon transferred from Monroe to act as receiver (the agent who

159

Woodworth's "Steamboat Hotel" in Detroit, where many pioneers heading west spent their first night in Michigan Territory.

160

accepted payment for lands) and Abram Edwards became register of claims.

The land office brought boom times to White Pigeon. Homesteaders queued up in front of the building, anxious to learn if the lands they lusted after were still available. Horsemen raced into town in a swirl of dust minutes ahead of rival claimants.

Most were bona fide settlers, eager to acquire their own farmsteads at $1.25 an acre. But a good number were speculators who sought to purchase large sections of valuable land for a song, or better yet, to pick town sites that could be platted into lots, then promoted and sold for hundreds or thousands of times their original cost. Wealthy eastern capitalists formed syndicates to invest in cheap Michigan land and sent agents into the wilderness to select prime sites. Rough-clad frontiersmen with their families and all worldly possessions in tow, land lookers, and shrewd townsite developers daily tramped the dusty street before White Pigeon's land office.

If the walls of this last surviving structure to have been used as a federal land office in Michigan could talk, what stories of heroic ventures, of dreams realized, or of hopes dashed might they tell. No sooner had the land office opened when Lucius Lyon, a deputy surveyor general who would become Michigan's first U.S. senator in 1837, arrived to buy what he considered some choice town sites. He ultimately acquired land in what is now downtown Battle Creek, Schoolcraft, Kalamazoo, and Grand Rapids.

White Pigeon surveyor Robert Clark Jr. and another speculator named J.J. Guernsey also purchased land at the confluence of the Kalamazoo River and a creek called the Battle. When Sands McCamly, who also saw the water power potential of this site, arrived at the land office, he found all the property already taken. But for some reason, Lucius Lyon and Robert Clark lost interest in developing Battle Creek and sold out to McCamly. He went on to put the

Lucius Lyon, surveyor, town site developer and Michigan's first U.S. senator.

town on the map and his own name on a major street.

Titus Bronson, an eccentric potato grower from Connecticut, arrived at the land office in 1831 to purchase a likely spot for a town. He and his brother-in-law took title to 160 acres of land where the Arcadia Creek ran into the Kalamazoo River. Lucius Lyon also invested in the site that Bronson named after himself. Later settlers renamed the thriving village Kalamazoo. Disgruntled, the old pioneer pulled up stakes and headed further west.

Other investors who named towns after themselves, including George Gale and Horace Comstock, also showed up at the White Pigeon land office. Chief among the advantages sought by town platters was designation as the county seat. Unfortunately for him, young Comstock was away on business when the commissioners charged with determining Kalamazoo's county seat arrived. Bronson, on the other hand, was there to give them a personal tour of his holdings, including the several blocks in the center he generously offered for public use. Kalamazoo won the courthouse sweepstakes. Comstock shifted his hopes to Allegan County and was soon back in White Pigeon to register land in what became the promising settlement of Otsego.

A French fur trader named Louis Campau arrived at the land office on September 19, 1831, to register a plat of land situated at the foot of the rapids on the Grand River where he had traded with the Indians for years. Again, Lyon bought an adjacent parcel. A long and bitter rivalry developed between these two co-founders of Grand Rapids.

In 1833 a coterie of eastern investors organized the Boston Company to purchase land in Allegan County. They hired George Ketchum of Marshall and Stephen Vickery and Anthony Cooley, both of Kalamazoo, to select land and register it at White Pigeon. They chose a prime site on a horseshoe bend of the Kalamazoo River which, with the assistance of Elisha Ely and his son, Alexander, of

An eccentric potato grower from Connecticut, Titus Bronson, founded Kalamazoo. (courtesy, Kalamazoo Public Museum)

Rochester, New York, became the village of Allegan.

The year that saw the genesis of Allegan also marked an important occasion for White Pigeon. In 1833 John Defrees moved his press from South Bend, which had lost out to Elkhart in being named the federal land office for northern Indiana. He selected what he thought would be a more likely location - White Pigeon. In December of 1833, Defrees published the first issue of the *Michigan Statesman and St. Joseph Chronicle* in White Pigeon. It was the first Michigan newspaper to be published west of Detroit.

A number of literary travelers penned impressions of White Pigeon in 1833. Charles Fenno Hoffman, a one-legged author making an equestrian tour of the west, arrived in December and thought it "quite a pretty village of four years' growth." He spent the night at Savery's "Old Diggins" tavern where he learned that a great number of English emigrants had settled on the prairie and, in true English fashion, had planted live hedges as fences.

Two British authors traveling by stage across Michigan in September of 1833, also stopped for the night in White Pigeon. Joseph Latrobe marveled that the entire prairie had been completely occupied by 160 farms within four years.

His traveling companion, Patrick Shirreff, had not enjoyed what he had seen thus far of Michigan, but he found more to his liking at White Pigeon. After breakfasting on a fine broiled ruffed grouse shot on the adjacent prairie, he took a stroll around the little settlement. He discovered a "small, pretty village, comprised of well-painted frame houses."

Harriet Martineau, a British lady who came through by stage in 1836, found White Pigeon Prairie "highly cultivated and looking just like any other rich and perfectly level land." After breakfasting at White Pigeon, she recorded: "We saw the rising ground where the Indian chief

Traveling writer Charles Fenno Hoffman, penned
descriptions of Michigan in 1833.

lies buried, whose name has been given to the place." Later, residents would erect a boulder monument at that site to commemorate their community's aboriginal namesake.

By the time of Mrs. Martineau's visit, much of the better land in the southern tier of counties had been taken. The mad rush for Michigan land had shifted to the north. As a result, the federal land office was relocated to Kalamazoo in 1834. Just before that, Defrees had sold his newspaper to an itinerant printer named Henry Gilbert. In 1835 Gilbert followed the land office to Kalamazoo where his paper eventually evolved into the *Kalamazoo Gazette*.

White Pigeon remained a vital village during the 19th century, its development spurred by the arrival of the Michigan Southern Railroad in 1851. It would experience its ups and downs, natural disasters, fires, economic evolution and, through it all, the old land-office building slumbered. The restoration and dedication of this momento of Michigan's cradle days in 1989 has preserved for future generations a vital reminder of their colorful heritage.

Factory Belles of Kalamazoo

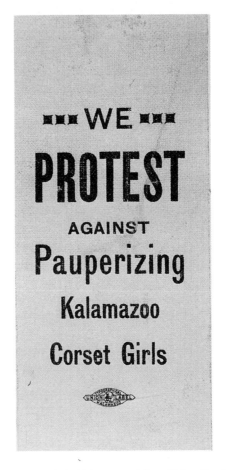

This reminder of the 1912 Kalamazoo strike which attracted national attention was worn by factory belle supporters.

The little bell that jingled each time a shopper opened the door to Clark and Babcock's fashionable Kalamazoo dry goods store rang a merry tune in April, 1855.

But most customers came not so much to finger the bolts of calico that lined the shelves as to catch a glimpse of two unusual employees. The Kalamazoo proprietors had attempted a daring break with tradition.

"We are pleased to see Clark and Babcock introducing female clerks," noted *Kalamazoo Gazette* editor Volney Hascall in the paper's April 5 edition. But in an era when the majority believed that "a woman's place is in the home," and professional women were to be found mainly in saloons and street corners few other Kalamazooans shared Hascall's liberal reaction.

The record fails to preserve even the names of these Kalamazoo pioneer female employees. Yet despite social stigmas, ogling customers, and unequal pay, their modest entry into the workplace launched a revolution.

When 1861 brought the Civil War and brother fought brother for four bloody years, home-front activities, rested increasingly on sister's shoulders. By the 1880s as the Celery City emerged as a burgeoning industrial center in southwest Michigan, factory needs brought recruitment of more and more lady laborers.

Popular American journals warned in 1887 that "there is growing a widespread neglect of and opposition to marriage because women are beginning to find out they can support themselves," and "the present effort of women to invade the higher forms of labor is battling with the established order of sexual relations, and the Almighty has established bounds beyond which woman cannot go without defeating the primary object of her creation."

But neither such logic nor the Almighty's bounds would prevent capitalists from hiring the cheapest workers they could get - women.

In 1895, the Michigan Bureau of Labor compiled a list of

56 occupations in which women worked, ranging from casket works to whip factories. In Kalamazoo, female factory workers fashioned items representative of the city's industrial diversity, including cigars, candy, corsets, paper, pills and pants.

As a matter of fact, during the 1890s most Kalamazoo factory females plied the rather traditional task of seamstress. By the end of the decade, 102 women worked at the Kalamazoo Pant and Overall shop, another 48 made similar products for S. Salomon and Co. and 90 women sewed silk bunting on masonic regalia at Henderson Ames. John McLarty employed 45 expert seamstresses at the French Skirt Co. to fashion his novel ready-made petticoats, while another 200 women toiled ten-hour days at the Featherbone Corset Co. to turn out essential - though "unmentionable" - Victorian apparel.

In the dawn of the 20th century, a flood of men poured from America's rural regions to seek their living in urban industrial centers. Women also said goodbye to the hoe and milk pail to join factory payrolls. Kalamazoo's population grew by 62 percent to 39,437 during the first decade of the century.

In 1910 the Michigan Bureau of Labor estimated that 186,183 women were "engaged in gainful occupations throughout the state," a 200 percent increase over 1900. By 1914, a special commission on the status of women workers pegged Kalamazoo's female workforce at 5,000. But - as more and more women timed their day by factory whistles - gains in wages, working conditions, and social status, as we shall see, lagged far behind.

Kalamazoo's largest employer of females during the pre-World War I era was by far the Kalamazoo Corset Co. In 1911, 833 women reported to the "world's largest corset factory," located at the northeast corner of Eleanor and Church streets.

The company originated in Three Oaks in Berrien County

A bevy of Kalamazoo Paper Company belles in 1923 (courtesy, W.M.U. Archives).

in the early 1880s when an imaginative entrepreneur, W.K. Warren, fashioned a substitute for whalebone out of splintered turkey feathers. Warren's featherbone proved an ideal replacement for the expensive whalebone required for corset stays. Soon puffing locomotives pulled long trains of boxcars loaded with turkey feathers as well as passenger cars packed with female job-seekers into the Berrien County hamlet. In 1893, James H. Hatfield relocated an offshoot of the featherbone industry, the Featherbone Corset Co., in Kalamazoo. Hatfield's enterprise grew rapidly and soon changed its name to the Kalamazoo Corset Co.

It was a highly competitive business. Rival corset-makers sought to beguile consumers with ever-changing fashions. By 1895 the Kalamazoo Corset Co. merchandised 20 styles available in varying colors and materials ranging from cheap cloth "jean" to silk batiste and brocade. Ladies could purchase corsets with high busts or low busts, depending on their own sense of propriety. Special lightweight "dancing corsets" contained little boning.

By the 1890s, corset-making had become a sophisticated craft. The hundreds of Kalamazoo women who reported each morning to the Kalamazoo Corset factory or its smaller local rival, the Puritan Corset Co., spent a long ten-hour day engaged in one of the 40 operations required to produce a corset. They cut material, stitched, joined seams, attached front clasps and back stitching, applied steel wires and boning, sewed eyelets, added draw strings, lace embroidery, or flossing, ironed corsets, tied little bows and sewed them on, put in hooks, eyes and lacing joined the two corset halves, and packed the finished corsets' in boxes to be shipped across the country.

Kalamazoo's corset-makers toiled six days a week to craft the products that molded America's fashionable "Gibson Girl" figures. Sixty hours a week, they lived with the bright glare of naked light bulbs hanging over their work, with the whir and clatter of rooms full of sewing machines, and with the creaking wheels of carts piled high with glistening corsets pushed by men from one work station to the next.

Despite the fact that Kalamazoo's average pay scale was one of the best in the state for the corset industry, women workers took home a wage pitiful by modern standards. A turn-of-the-century poll by the Michigan Bureau of Labor revealed that Kalamazoo women earned an average of 80 cents for a ten-hour day making corsets. They made ten cents more a day than women working at the American Card factory. The ladies who sorted rags at the various paper mills got only 67 cents for their ten hours. Male factory workers earned an average of $1.75 a day at this time, more than twice the wages for women.

Since wages were computed by the piece rate in the corset industry what a woman found in her pay envelope depended on her speed, skill and luck. Typically, employers charged workers for the thread, needles, and scissors they used. Fining was another widespread practice. A proportion of earnings might be deducted for tardiness, defective corsets, dropped stitches, or for sewing machine oil on the garments. The Michigan Bureau of Labor polled more than 800 women workers across the state and found that 50 percent had been fined for such infractions in their corset plants.

Conditions were ripe for unionization and the 20th century witnessed the organization of a variety of locals. But initial efforts to bring women's wages and working conditions into line with their male counterparts brought little success.

In 1901, 40 women and girls went on strike at the Kalamazoo Pant and Overall plant over a change in the piece-rate structure. Contemporary sympathy went to the "scores of men thrown out of employment because of the strike" and the women went back to work with little gained.

A Kalamazoo Corset Company ad from 1914 promoted the
instruments of torture produced by and for women.

Strikes became increasingly a way of life in Kalamazoo as the years passed. A series of strikes in 1908 by local cigar makers drove Kalamazoo's two largest cigar factories out of the city.

By 1912 the International Ladies Garment Workers Union (ILGWU) had become firmly established at the Kalamazoo Corset Co. Nearly 500 employees belonged to local 82. In February of 1912, the union sought a new contract that set the minimum wage for women at $7 a week and reduced the work week to 54 hours. Kalamazoo Corset President James H. Hatfield not only refused to negotiate but fired the entire union bargaining team.

Josephine Casey, firebrand ILGWU organizer, arrived from New York City to stir up the situation and about 500 corset workers went out on strike. Hatfield continued production with about 300 non-union employees and the union set up picket lines. When picketers got rowdy and harassed non-striking workers, Hatfield secured a court injunction against them.

Strikers changed their tactics and met each day for a half hour of prayer. Casey's silent picketing" drew national attention to the Kalamazoo Corset Co. strike. Kalamazooans held mass meetings and staged parades to support the strikers, but Hatfield held firm.

As strikers began gradually to give up the cause and return to work, Casey renewed picketing. Police raided the picket line and arrested six women, including Casey, and three men. Convicted of contempt of court, they each spent 36 days in jail. As the situation worsened, Mayor Charles B. Hayes convinced a local Methodist minister, Dr. W.M. Puffer, to mediate. On June 15, 1912, the union ended the three-and-half-month strike with a wage pact that guaranteed $5 a week.

In 1914, Hatfield reorganized the Kalamazoo Corset Co. to bring out a new line of "Madame Grace" corsets and formed another firm, the National Corset Co. (NACO).

Business boomed for the two factories until the boyish look of the 1920s flapper era ended the hourglass figure and the demand for corsets. NACO failed in 1929, but Kalamazoo Corset, renamed the Grace Corset Co., survived until 1957 by catering to overweight women who still needed a little girdling.

However, women factory workers at the turn of the century had a hard time getting plump. Skimpy wages, hard work, and long hours were their lot. Even the 30 to 50 women who dipped chocolates, shaped nut clusters, and packed bon-bons at the Hanselman Candy Factory on East Michigan Avenue stayed slim. They took home as little as $4 for a 60-hour work week in 1915 and usually faced layoffs after the holiday season.

Women lucky enough to get a job at one of the city's ten cigar factories fared a little better because of unionization. In 1904 more than 50 ladies helped roll 15 million Little Beauty, Big Heart, La Zoo, Wolverine Girl, Game Trout, and Miss Kazoo cigars.

They stripped stems from tobacco leaves, sorted the tobacco into grades, "bunched" the cheaper filler tobacco in binder leaf, and packed the cigars into wooden molds. They took home an average of 90 cents for an eight-hour day. Their male counterparts averaged $2.45 for the same time.

Cigar-making was traditionally a male-dominated trade, but because women could do the same work for far cheaper wages and could do it better in many cases, they had almost entirely supplanted men in Michigan by 1913. Throughout the state, the cigar-making industry employed the largest percentage of women under 16 (13 percent). Another 24 percent were between the ages of 16 and 18.

Employers, of course, worked out elaborate justifications for the unequal pay scales. "Women," a corpulent employer would explain, "didn't need to make as much as a man because they were not the chief

Teenaged women and boys labored at Lilies Cigar Company in Kalamazoo ca. 1900 (courtesy W.M.U. Archives).

breadwinner of a family." Most Americans believed that they were only working until they could find a husband and return to their natural role as housewife. And their cost of living was very low because they lived at home with their parents, or should anyway.

"Women need work as well as men, but they are willing to work for less because they can live on less and because they can live at home," concluded the Michigan State Commission of Inquiry into the Status of Working Women in 1914. The commission found that only ten percent of working women were married throughout the state and that 75 percent lived at home. A large percentage gave all their earnings to parents for family expenses and so "were ignorant of how much their living cost." This, the commission concluded, was one reason why so many women were satisfied to work for "a less than living" wage.

While living at home might inhibit the development of a financial sense, the commission thought if far wiser from a moral standpoint. To live "without the environment of a home" was to be "adrift." Some employers openly expressed preference for girls to live at home, frankly admitting, sniffed the commission, "that the wages offered did not permit a girl to live honestly elsewhere."

A female inspector journeyed to Kalamazoo in 1914 to document the living conditions available to the city's 5,000 working women. Rooms rented for $1 to $3.50 per week. Separate bathrooms were unheard of and usually a toilet was shared with other boarders of both sexes. Many landlords refused to rent to women because of the moral issue of entertaining boyfriends. Where she lived concluded the inspector, could "mean either the redemption or the downfall of a girl."

Working women, polled regarding the minimum income needed to survive in 1914, thought $10 a week necessary. One replied, "Before I received $10 a week, I often went to bed hungry." Another allowed that "a girl can live on less than $10 a week if she has a friend to take her to places of amusement."

That same year, 40 members of the Kalamazoo Ladies Library Association agreed that a wage-earning women needed to make $8.50 a week "to maintain her health in Kalamazoo." They budgeted $260 a year for room and board, $70 for clothes, $20 for doctors and dentists, 50 cents a week for trolley fares (five cents a ride then), 50 cents a week for laundry, 25 cents a week for recreation, ten cents a week for books and magazines, and ten cents a week for the collection plate at church. The members of the Kalamazoo Twentieth Century Club thought $10 a week was more accurate, but then they budgeted an extra $10 a year for new hats.

Few Kalamazoo employers thought a minimum-wage law to guarantee women a living wage was a very good idea in 1914. A representative of the Henderson Ames Co., which employed 195 women, thought a minimum wage would "place a premium on inefficiency and incompetency." "An ample wage can be earned," he assured, "if the worker takes reasonable advantage of her opportunity."

A few years earlier, Henderson Ames paid an average daily wage of only $1 to all employees. The minimum wage proposal brought this reaction from a spokesman for the Kalamazoo Loose Leaf Binder Co.: "It would be detrimental to the women of the state because, if compelled to pay higher wages, men would be employed who could do more work [the] women [would be] laid off."

While a turn-of-the-century female laborer might toil a ten-hour day and still not earn enough to keep from going to bed hungry, life at the factory had other drawbacks as well. Working conditions were often unsanitary and humiliating. The 1914 State Commission of Inquiry emphasized the necessity for eliminating dirty factory conditions. Work areas were filthy, ventilation often poor, and toilet facilities were "indecent and immoral and not up

These women who toiled in the Kalamazoo Paper Company ca. 1906 earned less than 7 cents an hour (courtesy, W.M.U. archives).

to 20th century standards." The commission reported that toilets for men and women were separated by thin partitions "reaching neither to the floor nor the ceiling," toilet paper hung outside the door, and toilets were located so that all in the factory could "see who entered or departed simply to save toilet paper."

When queried about toilet conditions in 1913 typical answers by Michigan factory women included, "no toilet paper whatever, no towels," "haven't been to the toilet, don't like to go," the man who cuts is always standing near." Another described the factory toilet as "just boards with holes emptying down into the river, boys can look up from downstairs."

When the factory-inspection law went into effect in Michigan in 1893 a team of inspectors similar to modern Occupational and Safety Health Administration personnel began touring Michigan factories, citing deficiencies. While the law had few teeth, the factory inspector published his citations in widely circulated annual reports which must have been a source of embarassment, at least, to offenders. Kalamazoo firms received citations for typical offenses. In 1899, the factory inspector found girls between the ages of 14 and 16 working at the Kalamazoo Corset Co., Henderson Ames, and the Kalamazoo Paper Co. The Electric Steam Laundry, Kalamazoo Pant and Overall, the French Garment Co., and S. Salomon and Co. were cited for unsuitable toilets.

In 1903, Deputy Inspector Herrington "found many violations of child labor" in the city of Kalamazoo. The employer, reported Herrington, was not always to blame because he was "confronted with sworn statements as to age, issued by a notary, for children under 14 years of age." He also uncovered false sworn statements by parents as to ages of their working children.

The year 1909 saw citations for unsanitary toilets for women issued to Ihling Bros. Everard, the Kalamazoo

Playing Card Co., El Merado Cigar Co., Illinois Envelope Co., and four other Kalamazoo firms. The inspector ordered Bryant Paper Co. to hang a door on the women's toilet and discharge a 13-year-old girl. He told the Columbia Hotel to "provide heat in the rooms of your female employees during winter months." In 1911, the Sanitary Laundry was given a week to place the women's toilet in "proper sanitary condition."

The state factory inspector sometimes discovered potentially more dangerous situations in the factories. In 1909, he ordered Kalamazoo's Rosenbaum and Sons Co.: "Do not lock, bolt or fasten any door during working hours leading from rooms where females are employed." Two years later 146 women workers would lose their lives in the Triangle Shirtwaist fire in New York City. Many were trapped because of similarly bolted doors.

During an age when society as a whole enjoyed far less time for leisure and recreation than today, working women had little in which to look forward. In 1914 only 20 percent of the state's working women received a paid vacation; 35 percent took no vacation at all.

When queried concerning their leisure activities a sampling of working women replied: "I don't know the meaning of the words amusement and recreation. I have all I can do to earn enough to live on;" "All I want when night comes is rest. When you work all day you don't feel much like amusement;" and ""I can't afford amusements and go without them, unless a friend takes me."

In 1904 the Women's Union Label League, No. 77, of Kalamazoo responded this way to a questionaire concerning what kind of labor legislation was needed the most: "A universal eight-hour day, more stringent child labor laws, laws requiring more sanitary work shops, and a law prohibiting women and girls working more than four hours without rest or more than eight hours in any 24."

More than eight decades later, women have become an

essential part of the work force. Many of the primitive working conditions once common have been improved. Forty-hour work weeks are the norm, wages are better, and toilets certainly are cleaner. Although other problems exist for working women, the workplace is a far cry from that of the "Good Old Days."

Bares in the Woods

Depression era Nudists enjoy a lively game of volleyball.

The old man slapped a deer fly off his sun-tanned rump, wagged his waist-length beard in satisfaction and leaped high to spike the volleyball over the net.

Nearby, two young ladies practiced dramatic poses *a la* Isadora Duncan. Some 20 other men, women, and children played games, chatted, or napped in the sun.

All had one thing in common - they were naked as the day they were born.

It was Labor Day, September 4, 1933, and the Sun Sports League had gathered at its remote camp located approximately six miles northwest of Allegan to enjoy the holiday weekend, *au naturel*. Fred and Ophelia Ring of Kalamazoo had opened the nudist colony six months before. They had picked a site that seemed to offer complete security for their eccentric practices.

The 55-acre tract lay three-quarters of a mile downstream from where Swan Creek passes under old M-89, now 118th Avenue. Dense second-growth oak, white pine, and sassafras surrounded three sides of an open three-acre compound. To the east a steep bluff ran down to Swan Creek. An impenetrable swamp lay between the fast-flowing little stream and another high bank 150 yards away.

Had one of the nudists taken a break from cavorting to glance at the ridge to the east, he might have caught a mirror-like glint in the underbrush. There, Allegan County Sheriff Fred Miller squatted in the brush, his field glasses trained on the camp.

The rural lawman, whose normal caseload involved fence disputes and stray animals, was getting quite an eyeful. He swatted a mosquito on his neck and handed the glasses to State Conservation Officer Harry Plotts. Had not the bugs been so bad this would have been pretty good duty. Then the peepers ducked back along the ridge to the highway where the posse waited.

Allegan County, as the nudists were about to discover,

was philosophically not an ideal locale for their modern Eden. Farmers dominated the population and times were bad down on the farm. Some of the county featured good land but the soil of much of the northwestern part, now the Allegan State Game Area, was little more than blow sand underlying a thin layer of forest mulch.

Unscrupulous real-estate agents had platted the cut-over pine land into little farmsteads and convinced gullible city dwellers to move back to the land. By the early 1930s, most of the little farms were up for tax sale.

As the Great Depression tightened its grip on the nation, Allegan County's bleak economic situation worsened. Michigan as a whole, heavily oriented to the automobile industry, was especially hard hit. Outstate rural communities, the bastion of Republicanism, fundamental religion, and agrarian conservatism, brooded over Franklin Roosevelt's revolutionary New Deal policies. In 1933, most Allegan County residents were in no mood for frivolity, much less nudists.

Since Eve first passed the apple to Adam and fig leaves became the fashion, strutting around in the buff had become somewhat less than socially acceptable. Modern-day nudists, of course, like to cite as precedents the naked aborigines living in a true state of nature, those found in an equatorial environment anyway.

History records other episodes of nudism. Old Testament Canaanites practiced baalism in the nude and an Egyptian pharoah, Ikhnaton, founded a religion that featured exposing the naked body to the sacred rays of the sun. When Alexander the Great invaded India, he encountered a set of gurus he named gymnosophists (naked sages). Spartan youths paraded nude in the streets and Roman athletes routinely wrestled in the raw. But for most later civilizations, clothes made the man.

By the Victorian era, etiquette prohibited even discussing nakedness. Table legs were limbs and underwear unmentionables. Victorians surreptitiously ogled nude statuary, but the real thing was taboo. Many American communities passed laws decreeing the proper length for male and female bathing attire. Well into the 1930s, it was illegal for a male to expose his chest at certain beaches.

Partially in reaction to stifling Victorian mores, a German philosopher, Richard Ungewitter, at the turn of the century wrote a book about the benefits of going naked. Soon another German, Paul Zimmerman, founded the world's first nudist resort. The idea caught on slowly but during the 1920s, Adolph Koch popularized a regime of nude gymnastics and sun bathing at his institute in Berlin. By 1926, 50,000 Germans actively practiced nudism.

The movement spread to other European countries and in 1929 a German emigrant, Kurt Barthel, and two other pioneer nudists met at a New York City restaurant, ordered a sauerkraut dinner, and proceeded to establish the first permanent nudist organization in America.

Soon a husband-and-wife writing team, Frances and Mason Merrill, published a best seller, *Among the Nudists.* A half dozen other heavily illustrated books on the subject fanned the cause among Americans.

Sometime in 1931, Fred Ring, a middle-aged Kalamazoo dance instructor, slight, stoop-shouldered, horn-rimmed glasses and all, became a convert to the nudist cause. His wife, Ophelia, a stylish blond prone to wearing the latest hats and carefully sculpted spit curls, followed suit.

When he aired his new beliefs in public, most Kalamazoo clients took their tango lessons elsewhere. Ring supplemented his declining dance trade with a job in the machine shop at the Illinois Envelope Company on Bryant Street. Ophelia tended the home fires.

By early 1933, the Rings had made up their minds to establish a nudist camp. Ophelia recalled that they "had driven thousands of miles seeking a secluded and otherwise

Typical Nudist ads from 1933.

188

desirable spot." They settled on Allegan County's Valley Township.

The Rings first negotiated with Mrs. Mary Angier of Wheaton, Illinois, to purchase a site on Swan Creek. When her price proved too high, they secured another tract on the opposite side of the creek from her property. Mrs. Angier reportedly swore they would be sorry for that.

On March 1, 1933, a few hardy nudists braved goose bumps and chilblains to pose for publicity photographs at the camp. As spring gave way to warmer weather and hordes of biting gnats, deer flies, "no-seeums," mosquitos, and an occasional gigantic horsefly competed for the nudists' blood, the Rings erected two small shacks for protection. Despite the insect foes, the colony prospered.

By-mid summer, the Sun Sports League membership roster stood at more than 40. Prospective members filled out a detailed questionnaire to demonstrate their "fitness for association with nudists and sympathy for the movement." Ring sought to keep out the "merely curious."

Mostly well-to-do married couples and singles drove from Kalamazoo, Ann Arbor, and Chicago for a weekend of fun in the sun. Ring charged 50 cents a weekend per person for the privilege of going naked in the woods. Guests supplied their own tents.

Despite no-trespassing signs around the periphery of the property and a locked gate at the entrance to the long, twisting drive that led to the encampment, the existence of the nudist colony become common knowledge in Allegan. A favorite Sunday drive that summer featured a trip out to Swan Creek to maybe catch a peek at a bare bottom or two.

Allegan historian John Pahl remembers in his boyhood intently peering off into the woods as the family idled by the property. In particular, when Mrs. Angier arrived to vacation at her Swan Creek property, she grew increasingly curious about her strange in-the-buff neighbors.

It's conceivable that the nudists might have remained unmolested on their private property had not Mrs. Angier instigated an investigation. She complained to Sheriff Miller about the strange goings-on across the creek. The value of her property was deteriorating, she insisted, because of the presence of a nudist colony.

State Conservation Officer Plotts was called in because she thought the nudists might set the woods on fire. Then again, maybe Mrs. Angier's complaints only added fuel to the fire. Perhaps other segments of the Allegan community had already decided that the nudists had to go. Regardless of the provocation, Miller and Plotts had seen enough through binoculars, they thought, to raid the camp without a search warrant of any kind.

Miller and Plotts worked their way back to the posse assembled on the highway and the raid was on. A Michigan State Police investigator, ironically named Murray Peek, two sheriff's deputies, Allegan County Prosecutor Welborne Luna, Mrs. Angier, several private citizens, and *Allegan News* editor Douglas Alcock brought the number of raiders to an even dozen. The posse followed Mrs. Angier up her side of the fence line, then charged up the bluff to the camp. Mary Angier, slightly heavy-set and 60 years old, scrambled up the steep bank with the best of them.

When the mob stormed into the compound, nudists scattered into the woods in every direction. Miller and his deputies began taking the names of those who had not retreated to the bush and briars. Meanwhile, editor Alcock snapped pictures as fast as he could. Fred Ring quickly donned an overcoat and Ophelia pulled a dress on over her head and they began parleying with the intruders. Old Mary Angier huffed into the camp too late to see Ring in the nude, but, as she later testified, she saw enough to realize the colony "was a menace to anyone wandering through my land."

Ring tried to pacify her to little avail with a promise to

Allegan jurors took a hike through the woods to inspect the Swan Creek Nudist colony site.

plant a row of evergreens to screen the property. Miller and his deputies threatened to take the nudists directly to jail "in the raw." But since there were no warrants of any kind prepared, no arrests were made. On their way out, Investigator Peek and the deputies jotted down the license-plate numbers of the nudists' vehicles and later got additional names and addresses from that source.

The day after the raid, Prosecutor Luna went to work with a vengeance. He secured arrest warrants for indecent exposure for the Rings. Seventeen other nudists and the couple's two juvenile daughters were also named in the bill of particulars. On Wednesday, the Rings voluntarily appeared in an Allegan court and were released after posting $100 bond. They were to appear on Saturday for arraignment before Allegan Justice of the Peace Fidus E. Fish.

The nudist-colony raid made the front page of the *Kalamazoo Gazette* on September 7, and again on September 10. Prosecutor Luna had dismissed all warrants except those against the Rings by the day of the arraignment.

The Rings appeared before Justice Fish to assert that their nudist activities could only have been discovered by "peeping toms" and demanded examination in the lower court on the charges. The examinations were set for September 21 and the Rings remained free on bond. Vowing to fight the case to the highest court, the nudists acted quickly to secure the best attorney Allegan had to offer.

They chose "courtroom ace" Clare E. Hoffman, who had lost few cases during his practice of more than 30 years. Hoffman's statewide reputation, his razor-keen mind and sense of humor packed courthouses wherever he went. Hoffman, destined to become a congressman, took the case but later admitted that he "did not believe in nudism...but contended that the present law was not merely to apply to an exhibition regardless of the intent."

Representatives of the press arrived *en masse* for the September 21 hearing. The *Chicago Tribune, Chicago Herald and Examiner*, the *Kalamazoo Gazette, Grand Rapids Press, Detroit Free Press*, and a New York tabloid sent reporters to Allegan.

Expecting a large crowd, Justice Fish moved the event from his second-floor downtown office to the circuit-court room in the majestic Allegan County courthouse. Fish, a renowned local jurist with 52 years of practice and leader of the local spiritualist community, made quite a hit with the Chicago reporters when he explained his theories on spirit communication to them. They followed him back to his office to see pictures of two of his favorite spirit controls, an Indian princess and Thomas Jefferson.

Despite the unusual nature of the case, few local spectators showed up. The good old Allegan County Fair was running strong that week with special midway features. Other sensation seekers might have traveled to the Chicago World's Fair, where Sally Rand and her fan were stirring up a controversy along similar lines. Those who opted for either fair missed some interesting testimony.

So interesting, in fact, that Prosecutor Luna made his wife, who normally served as his secretary, stay in another room during explicit nudism testimony. Luna presented a surprise witness, Edward J. Murray of Chicago. Murray, who for some reason had joined the nudist colony to cure his high blood pressure, turned traitor because Ring had promised him it was legal, and it obviously was not.

Defense attorney Hoffman made short work of the surprise witness, called him a Judas and threatened to seek a warrant for Murray on his own testimony. Chicago correspondent Robert McHaffery noted that following his testimony, Murray "grabbed his hat and disappeared."

After Peek, Miller, and Mrs. Angier took the stand, Hoffman moved to drop the charges because the camp had

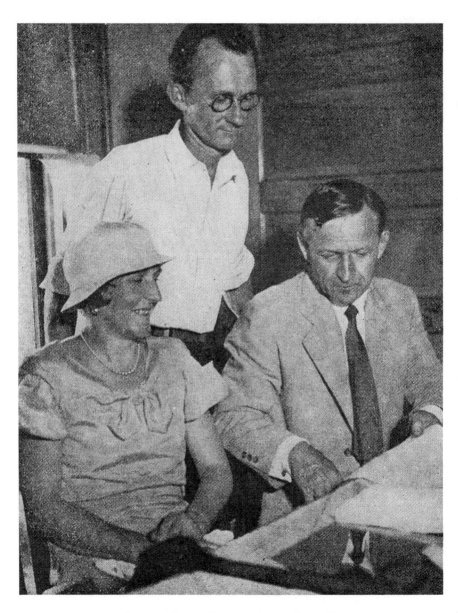

Attorney Clare Hoffman, seated, confers with
Fred and Ophelia Ring during their trial.

been closed since the raid. Justice Fish overruled the motion and bound the Rings over for the October session of the circuit court. They darted out of the court-room, late for their guest appearance at a nudist publicity film being shown at Kalamazoo's Fuller Theatre.

By the time of the court date, charges had been dropped against Ophelia Ring as Luna decided to concentrate on convicting Fred Ring of indecent exposure. The Reverend Ilsley Boone, American nudist pioneer and managing editor of *The Nudist*, arrived from New York City to view the court proceedings in October. He published his observations in the December, 1933, issue of *The Nudist*. Boone applauded the press coverage accorded the trial with the exception of the *Allegan Gazette*. Editor Alcock,it seems, had thought the pictures he had taken at the nudist colony too indecent for his own journal, but he sold them at a profit to other newspapers.

Hoffman, with the assistance of Kenneth Krippene, a Chicago attorney and legal representative of the International Nudist Conference, handled the trial masterfully, but they apparently had little chance of winning in the Allegan arena. Circuit Court Judge Fred T. Miles of Holland openly admitted his belief that nudism "was not and could not be anything but deliberate exhibitionism for lewd purposes." The trial reminded some observers of the Salem witchcraft proceedings.

At the onset of the trial, Hoffman moved for dismissal, citing the constitutional right of private property and due process of law including the fact that the evidence had been gathered without search warrants. He next moved for a change of venue because the jury, made up of local farmers, had been intimately associating with members of the raiding posse. Judge Miles quickly overruled both motions.

At Ring's insistence, Hoffman based his defense on the health and mental hygiene benefits of nudism. He called

Dr. John R.C. Carter of Detroit to the stand. Carter was the state's leading authority on solar-ray therapy. Luna objected to Carter's testimony because he had not been at the camp on the day of the raid. Judge Miles sustained the objection and ruled that no further testimony along that line could be introduced.

When Judge Miles presented his charge to the jury, he left little chance for a verdict of innocence. If Fred Ring exposed himself deliberately, he did so obscenely and indecently, the judge instructed. The jury soon returned their verdict - guilty. On November 18, Judge Miles sentenced Fred Ring to 60 days in the county jail, a fine of $300, and court costs of $53.79. In passing sentence, he addressed the defendant:

"You knew - you must certainly have known - that if you came into this quiet, decent, law-abiding community and did as you did, that you would shock everyone's sense of decency. I can't help believing that you intended to do so . .

You have played up your wrongdoing in the public press and on the degenerate stage. You have tried to make people believe that you are martyrs to pure air and sunshine. Perhaps you have succeeded in deceiving yourself. I should not like to believe you have deceived others.

It is hoped that the public reaction to your immoral conduct is such that no person, be he ever so degenerate, will attempt to follow your example."

Ring appealed his case to the Michigan Supreme Court. The appeal dragged on for six months. The Reverend Boone sought donations for the Ring defense fund in his magazine. On June 4, 1934, the Michigan Supreme Court affirmed Judge Miles' decision. "A nudist colony," Chief Justice J. Bushnell ruled, "was not the same as a defendant's house or castle." Ring, who loved sunshine so well, spent the better part of the summer of 1934 in one of the narrow, airless cells in the old brick jail on Allegan's Walnut Street. Martyr or not, he became the first nudist in America to go

The scene of the 1933 Nudist trial, the majestic Allegan County courthouse was razed in 1961.

to jail for his beliefs.

Nudism had gone on trial in five other states previous to the Ring decision, but no more than a nominal conviction had been secured in any case. However, Michigan's judicial precedent ushered in a wave of nudist persecution.

Late in 1934, Governor Al Smith sponsored a bill that outlawed nudism in New York state. A series of legal incidents in Michigan, Indiana, and Ohio followed passage of the "Al Smith Law." During the late 1930s and 1940s, lawmen located several nudist enclaves through the use of low-flying aircraft and promptly raided them. The midwest became a nudist's No-Man's-Land.

On June 30, 1956, police swept into Sunshine Gardens, a 140-acre nudist camp near the outskirts of Battle Creek. This particularly brutal raid, during which the police roughed up some of the nudists, had been promoted by Braxton Bragg Sawyer, a local radio revivalist. The case was ultimately appealed to the Michigan Supreme Court. Justice John Voelker, better known by his literary pseudonym Robert Traver, swayed the bench to issue a landmark judgment that exonerated the nudists and censored the police for their conduct. *People vs. Ring* had been finally overturned.

After serving the 60-day jail sentence, Fred Ring had returned to his job at the Illinois Envelope Company. Apparently, by 1938 enough of the community had forgotten his crime to enable Ring to start instructing dance again. Throughout the late 1930s and the war years, he alternately taught dance and worked for the envelope company. Fred and Ophelia Ring never reopened the Swan Creek nudist colony.

Justice Fidus E. Fish, jurist and spiritualist medium of note, suddenly dropped dead while engaged in public debate on December 4, 1933. Welborne Luna remained Allegan County Prosecutor until 1938 and Fred Miller kept his sheriff's badge through 1940. Judge Fred Miles continued to serve as circuit court judge for the counties of Allegan and Ottawa until 1947.

The Ring trial would be Clare Hoffman's last major courtroom appearance. In June 1934, he announced his candidacy as Republican nominee for the Fourth Congressional District. He unseated incumbent Democrat George Foulkes of Hartford in November. Hoffman went on to win the next 14 elections to become one of the most powerful Republican congressmen in Washington, earning the nickname "The Lone Eagle."

Mary Angier returned to Wheaton, Illinois. By the late 1930s, her Swan Creek property had reverted to the state of Michigan. Her tract and the site of the nudist colony became part of the Allegan State Forest which had been established in 1935. Civilian Conservation Corps workers converted the nudist colony into a picnic area and campground. Generations of local Boy Scouts told their parents they were going camping at the nudist colony.

When the Michigan Department of Natural Resources changed the designation and purpose of the Allegan State Forest to the Allegan State Game Area, the campground was closed. Now overgrown and hidden, the site of the nudist -colony raid that focused national attention on Swan Creek, Valley Township, and Allegan has slipped into oblivion.

The Great Tomato Scare: Cancer Cure Charlatans in Michigan

Beware the poisonous fruit.

℘rofessor E.S. Dunster of the University of Michigan College of Medicine sadly shook his head one day in 1878 as he described "The Case of the Intemperate Nurse." No, it was not overuse of alcohol or narcotics that brought about her downfall - it was bingeing on raw tomatoes.

"Why, she would eat them raw, in season and out of season, as freely as we would eat fruit," the professor recalled. "I remember that while attending a patient in my own family, her breakfast was almost invariably prefaced with two or three large raw tomatoes. This free use of the vegetable she kept up for years. She died at Roosevelt Hospital in New York City," Dunster paused so that the full effect of the horror of the results of her intemperance would sink in, then he whispered, "of cancer of the uterus, of over a year's duration."

Although the professor had taken precaution as a scientist to preface his story with the caveat that "it very likely was only a coincidence," his citing of the nurse's case in answer to a statewide query concerning the "causal connection between the very general use of tomatoes for the last 10 or 20 years, and the apparent increase in the number of cancerous affections" placed him squarely astride the fence on the issue. Furthermore, he admitted "I frequently meet with this idea among people even very intelligent and well informed."

Michigan and much of the Midwest was, in fact, experiencing a great tomato scare in the late 19th Century. Where modern researchers would, undoubtedly, feed massive quantities of the pulpy red fruit to laboratory rats, Dr. Homer O. Hitchcock of Kalamazoo sought to get to the root of the issue by polling his professional brethren. Hitchcock, a former president of the Michigan State Medical Society and founder of the State Board of Health, received 60 replies to his questionnaire from doctors across the state.

While the physicians' consensus largely exonerated the

Dr. Homer O. Hitchcock, who got to the root of the great tomato scare.

tomato as the cancer-causing culprit, they were far from in agreement as to the actual reasons for the increase in the number of cancer cases.

Hitchcock, himself, thought it likely that cancerous diseases of the stomach were caused by "the fact that many people take their food and drink so very hot, and also that the majority of people bolt their food without mastication, and in the shortest possible time."

Hitchcock also sided with Dr. A.L. Padfield of St. Clair who was inclined to blame "the growth of intemperate habits, in the use of tobacco, and alcoholic liquors . . . and the increased indulgence of promiscuous sexual intercourse."

Dr. Hal C. Wyman of Blissfield traced the origins of the tomato-causing-cancer theory to an article in the September 1871 *Eclectic Medical Journal* of Pennsylvania. It seems that a Professor J.D. Hylton had examined tomato cells under the microscope and found them to be identical in appearance to cancer cells. "If this fact is true and can be substantiated by other chemists," Hylton reported in his article, "it may in some manner account for the fearful increase of cancer in sections of the country where this fruit in cultivated."

Upon investigation, Hylton's scientific credentials proved to be those of a "miserable lifeless bantling," but then as now, rumors about cancer-causing agents spread like a prairie fire and were just as difficult to stamp out. For decades, many continued to shun the tomato, or "love apple" as it was once known, as poisonous.

Be it tomatoes, promiscuity or hurried eating, as imaginative as the theories were for cancer causes promoted by doctors and laymen alike during that era, equally bizarre were the many remedies advocated for the affliction.

Take, for example, that encyclopedia of folk wisdom compiled by good old Dr. Alvin W. Chase of Ann Arbor. Dr.

Chase's *Receipt Book and Household Physician* went through myriad editions, each more comprehensive than its predecessor, from the l860s until well into the 20th century, and achieved a reputation as a source of guidance second only to the *Bible*. The 1887 edition contained no less than eight "successful" home remedies for cancer. Should one method prove ineffective, Chase advised his readers to try another until they hit the right one - if they were still alive, that is.

Typical of Chase's cancer cures was the following: "Take equal parts of sweet fern and the bark off the north side of a black ash tree; burn both to ashes; leach and boil down; put a piece of sheet-lead upon the cancer, with a hole in it as large as the cancer, wet lint in the mixture; put on and place another piece of sheet-lead over that. Let it remain till it ceases to pain, when the cancer will be dead; then make a plaster of white-of-an egg and white pine pitch; put on and cover with a warm Indian (corn) meal poultice; keep on till it comes out. In the case of the man from whom this receipe was obtained, the cancer came out in nine days. The poultice must be renewed when cold."

Those sufferers who despaired of doctoring themselves might try their luck with any of the scores of cancer specialists whose advertisements flourished among the back pages of popular journals and newspapers of the period. It was the "Golden Age of Quackery" and America, long the land of entrepreneurs quick to capitalize on any of society's needs, spawned hordes of "cancer vampires" who preyed on their ailing countrymen's fears.

Dr. G.W. Topping, a reputable practitioner from DeWitt who had also responded to Hitchcock's 1878 tomato poll, in fact, thought "the apparent increase in cancerous affections largely due to the number of 'cancer doctors' who are traveling the country seeking whom they may pluck." He cited the case of a neighboring farmer whom a Professor Heber Claflin of the North Western Cancer Institute of

Dr. Alvin Chase of Ann Arbor spent a lifetime
collecting recipes and medical lore.

Chicago fleeced to the tune of $250 for removing a benign tumor the size of a pea from his face, assuring the farmer it was a "rose cancer" and very dangerous.

In Michigan, were the truth known, more than one prominent family's fortune was founded on patent-medicine huckstering and related medical shenanigans. Few, however, were as heartless as the technique practiced by the Mixer family of Hastings.

It was in 1864, so the Mixers' saga ran, that Dr. Charles W. Mixer contracted a vicious cancer that began "eating away his life." For nine long years he suffered while the cancer destroyed his nose, palate and portions of his face and throat. Then, miraculously, the good doctor discovered "the great remedy that cured him."

Even more miraculous, Dr. Mixer found his mysterious nostrum to be a veritable panacea that was good for a litany of ailments whose very names strike fear to this day, including goitre, catarrh, piles, salt-rheum, scald-heads and scrofula. As the decades rolled by and Mixer was joined by his son, Dr. S.S. Mixer, the two were able to "cure thousands who were threatened with operation and death" through doses of the Mixers' miracle medicines.

By 1909, newspapers across the nation carried the Mixers' eye-grabbing advertisements featuring the hideous cancer-ravaged face of the father flanked by the honest-appearing, manly visage of the son. "Thanks to his miraculous treatment," the ad assured readers, although horribly disfigured, the elder Mixer had "not suffered a day since its discovery." That statement was, beyond a shadow of a doubt, at least partially true. He had definitely not suffered during the preceeding six years - he died in 1903.

Be that as it may, as late as 1912 company promotional material still identified the elder Mixer as the firm's manager. The Mixers' pitch also included a generous supply of testimonials from doctors, lawyers, mechanics, ministers, laboring men, bankers, and every other occupation save that of Indian chief, it seems. Urged the Mixers' ad: "If you know of anyone who is afflicted with cancer, (or any of the other baker's dozen of diverse diseases their remedy was good for) you can do them a Christian act of kindness by sending us their addresses so we can write them how easily they can be cured in their own home."

Among those who responded to that amazing offer in July 1909 was a certain L.F. Kay, who in reality was Dr. F.P. Morgan of the U.S. Department of Agriculture's Pure Food and Drug Act Investigative Bureau. Morgan received a prompt reply from the Mixers informing him that they could "cure cancer without the knife or caustics by sending their patient certain medicines."

It was not even necessary for the afflicted to visit the good doctors in their Hastings office at 286 State Street. He or she need merely fill out the enclosed questionnaire and the doctors would "correctly diagnose the case and furnish the necessary treatment."

Morgan randomly checked certain boxes on the form, sent it in and promptly received his diagnosis. Sadly, he learned that he suffered from "cancer of the epithelial type." But happily, there was "no reason why you cannot be cured."

Morgan then mailed in the $11.80 requested for his first batch of medicine. That sum amounted to more than a week's wages for a factory worker of that era. He soon received a box bulging with seven different "treatments," including Mixer's Cancer and Scrofula Syrup, Cancer Reducer, Cancer Paste and Cancer Salve.

Morgan turned the entire lot over to Dr. C.H. Kimble, assistant chemist of the U.S. Drug Division, who took the liberty of analyzing their compositions. Kimble discovered the reducer to be a mixture predominantly of camphor and glycerin in a strong alcohol base, the paste to be vaseline, camphor and flaxseed, and the salve to contain vaseline, lanolin and powdered opium. The Mixers' best-selling shelf

A dead father and his quack son from Hastings
duped cancer sufferers with ads like this.

remedy, the syrup, turned out to be basically sarsaparilla and alcohol - in essence, root beer with a kick.

While it hardly seemed necessary, a body of reputable physicians convened a hearing and testified that the remedies "could not be relied on to effect the cure of any case of cancer, irrespective of the kind, duration or location."Further investigation revealed that the younger Mixer's credentials were as bogus as his treatments. A nationwide directory of physicians published in 1904 listed him as an "eclectic," that is, a member of a school of medical thought that let the patient, or next of kin, select whatever medicines they wanted. However, Mixer was found to be "neither a graduate of nor licensed to practice medicine." In other words, the Mixers' highly touted "cancer laboratory" was being operated by a dead man and a quack.

Upon recommendation from the assistant U.S. attorney general, in November 1909 Post Office authorities cited Mixer "to show why a fraud order should not be issued against his concern."

Mixer - the live one, that is, - was active in the Republican Party and an advanced-degree Mason, accomplishments not to be taken lightly in the southwestern Michigan of that era. He was not about to take this attack on his livelihood sitting down. Certain high-ranking friends in Washington promptly got Congress' Post Office Committee to launch a counter-investigation against the Post Office. The case dragged on into 1912, when, to make a long story short, the charges against Mixer were dropped.

He continued his cancer scam, although he took the precaution of rubber-stamping the title of "Dr." off his letterhead and other advertising. He also avoided sending his treatments through the U.S. mail. Instead, patients were directed to pick up their cancer cures at his Hastings office.

Mixer also continued to be a stalwart Republican Party

worker and was, in fact, appointed assistant sergeant-at
-arms to the 1912 Republican National Convention in
Chicago.   While in the Windy City, he encouraged local
cancer sufferers to visit him for a personal interview.

Back in Hastings, Mixer erected a large infirmary to the
rear of his residence at 414 South Jefferson Street, where,
during the ensuing decades gullible victims "by the
trainload" got his phony treatments.   Finally in 1934,
Mixer, at the age of 82, joined his father in whatever place
has been reserved for patent-medicine proprietors to spend
eternity.

Despite Mixer's successful dodging of the letter of the law
through his political connections, other cancer-cure frauds
did not fare so well in Michigan.   By 1913, thanks largely
to plenty of lurid publicity about quacks by the American
Medical Association Task Force and a "wide awake"
secretary of the State Board of Medical Registration,
Michigan authorities were able to crack down on a number
of other "cancer vampires."

W.J. Croziero, a notorious travelling quack who preyed
upon female sufferers in particular, found the small towns
of Michigan a lucrative field until he was arrested in Paw
Paw in October 1913 and fined $50 for illegal advertising.
Three years earlier he had applied for a license to practice
medicine in Michigan under the name of Crozier, claiming
to have been born in France.   Soon thereafter, however, he
added an "O" to his name and began billing himself as the
"Spanish Specialist in Chronic and Female Diseases."   He
was able to diagnose any disease without asking the patient a
single question.   He promised also to "cure cancer and
ulcers by electricity and blood machines."   Ultimately
finding Michigan "too hot for him," Crozier, alias Croziero,
slid over the line into Indiana and Illinois where he
continued his scams.

The year 1913 proved a banner one for the exposure of
quacks in Michigan.   In November 1913, the Rev. D. R.

Schiller was nabbed in Ionia for practicing medicine without a license. He pleaded guilty but was placed on probation for two years after promising to give up quackery and return to his home in Rockford, Illinois.

The story of Schiller - in reality, John F. Braum - and his wife and business partner, Kate, forms an interesting chapter in the annals of quackdom. In 1888, Braum had taken time out from his Red Bud, Illinois, photography business to enroll in a course in magnetic healing. Following graduation he and his wife took to the road with their telepathic healing enterprise. Billing themselves as Professor John F. Braum, "Himself," and Professor Kate A. Braum, "Herself," "the people you hear so much about" - the pair promised to cure all diseases, including cancer, without the use of drugs, surgery or even seeing the patient.

Taking the precaution to appear "for one day only" in a circuit of small midwestern towns, Braum, Himself and Herself, managed to stay a step ahead of numerous posses. That is, until 1903, when certain disgruntled parties in Nashville, Illinois, succeeded in laying hands upon Himself. He got out of that jam by paying a stiff fine. But the following year, a federal conviction for sending obscene advertising through the mails landed him in jail for six months.

Upon release, he continued to ply his quackery, a recidivism that brought him additional jail time, including a one year's stint in the Leavenworth Penitentiary. Braum, Herself, escaped incarceration because of her large brood of offspring, which ultimately numbered 10.

Even life in the federal prison failed to make an honest man of Braum. After paying his debt to society, Braum, under the appellation the Rev. D.R. Schiller, began hawking "blessed" handkerchiefs, which, when placed on affected portions of the anatomy, were guaranteed to produce a cure.

Eventually, however, Braum found Himself unable to merely sit by and let his wife enjoy all the fame and fortune of plucking sick suckers. In 1914, he made the mistake of writing a letter to a would-be assistant in which Braum urged him to grow a Van Dyke beard so that his "physiognomy would be in proper shape to look the patients in the eye and see how much money they have in their pockets."

That damning document wound up in the hands of a district attorney and Judge Kenesaw Mountain Landis, of later baseball commissioner fame, sentenced the old quack to four more years in Leavenworth. That seemed to have settled Himself's hash for good. However, the family persevered. In 1918, two of the Braum children were hauled into a Rochester, Indiana, courtroom for operating a psychic-healing practice under the aliases of Bonita and Oliver Rose.

The following year brought the advent of yet another Michigan-based bogus cancer cure, this time under the auspices of a genuine physician. In 1919, less than one year after he had received his medical diploma, 34-year-old Dr. William Kock of Detroit announced that he had "developed a real specific cure for cancer." Kock's cure was based on his belief that cancer was caused by a germ resembling the spirochete of syphilis. Despite three carefully controlled investigations by the Wayne County Medical Society, which found Kock's remedies to be worthless, he remained unconvinced. As late as 1936 he was widely advertising his "Glyoxylide" for the treatment not only of cancer but tuberculosis, psoriasis, leprosy, poliomyelitis and syphilis as well.

Such panaceas promoted by real doctors, however, lay outside the mainstream of cancer quackery. Most continued to be, like the Mixers, fraudulent father-and-son schemes. For example, from the tiny village of Garden, tucked away in the remote Upper Penninsula's Garden Peninsula, came the Lamotte Cancer Institute. The treatment, a paste made from secret herbs and roots, had been discovered by Edward

ANOTHER HOXIDE PATIENT DIES OF PNEUMONIA

W. N. Rodgers, 65, of Bonnie, near Mt. Vernon, died at 3 p. m. Tuesday at the Klondike hotel. He had been in this city five weeks receiving the Hoxide treatment for the removal of a cancer. His death is said to have been caused from pneumonia.

Mrs. Rodgers arrived here this morning accompanied by relatives. The body was shipped to Mt. Vernon, where funeral services and burial will take place.

OHIO WOMAN DIES HERE IN SANITARIUM

Miss Mary C. Tingle, 50 of Zanesville, O., died shortly after noon today at the Hoxide cancer sanitarium where she was receiving treatment for cancer of the liver. Before her entrance to the sanitarium on February 27, she had submitted to two operations.

Miss Tingle was born in Newport, Ky., Dec. 18,1875, the daughter of M. and Mrs. William T. Tingle. Until her illness she was employed as stenographer at the American Rolling company in Zanesville. She was a member of the Episcopal church of that city.

She leaves two sisters, Mrs. C. O. Snyder and Mrs. W. H. Neikirk both of Zanesville, the latter of whom is here with Miss Tingle.

The remains will be shipped this evening to Ohio, where funeral services and burial will take place.

DEATH A DAY WEEK'S RECORD AT THE HOXIDE

Death Certificates Show Pneumonia As Cause In Cancer Cases.

Mrs. Carrie Wolff, 66, of Sun Prairie, Wis., died at 3:20 o'clock Wednesday afternoon at the Hoxide cancer sanitarium, where she was receiving treatment for cancer. She came to this city, accompanied by her sister, Mrs. Mint Finger, and entered the sanitarium two months ago. According to the death certificate, her death resulted from pneumonia lobar.

Mrs. Wolff had resided in Sun Prairie her entire life, being born there on Nov. 17, 1859. She was a member of the Methodist church of that city.

Surviving are three sisters, Mrs. D. D. Vincent, Windsor, Wis,; Mrs. J. H. Wolf, Cottage Grove, Wis., and Mrs. Mint Finger, Sun Prairie, Wis.

The remains will be shipped to Wisconsin this evening and will be accompanied by Mrs. Finger.

Mrs. Wolff's death is the third this week at the Hoxide, one death occurring on each day.

CHICAGO MAN DIED HERE TODAY

Z. A. Davis, 73, of Chicago, died at 4:10 o'clock this morning at the Hoxide cancer sanitarium, where he had been receiving treatment the last two months for cancer of the lips.

The body was shipped at 10:38 this morning to Chicago, where funeral services and burial will take place.

M. SOWERS, OHIO, DIES HERE IN SANITARIUM

Marvin L. Sowers, died at 7:40 o'clock last night at the Hoxide Cancer sanatorium where he had been a patient since October 2. His death resulted from cancer of the left side of the face. Mr. Sowers came here last October from Circleville, O.

He is survived by his wife. The body will be shipped to Circleville, O. where funeral services and burial will take place.

J. L. JOHNSON, CLINTON, DIES AT HOTEL HERE

J. L. Johnson of Clinton, British Columbia, died at 9 o'clock last night at the Klondike hotel. He came to this city two weeks ago and was receiving treatment for cancer of the throat. It is said, his death resulted from pneumonia. He was about 72 years old.

The body was removed to the Connolly and Wallace Undertaking establishment pending word from relatives in British Columbia.

HOXIDE CANCER PATIENT DIES AT NOKOMIS

Mrs. Lillie Petty, wife of John Petty, died at her home in Nokomis, Thursday night of cancer of the breast one week after leaving the Hoxide Cancer sanitarium in this city where she had been taking treatment. She became afflicted with the disease about eight months ago.

Dr. Arthur Cramp assembled a collection of none too favorable Hoxie Clinic publicity in 1925

213

Lamotte, a man with no medical education. After the founder's death in 1925, Edward Lamotte Jr. followed in his father's footsteps. Four years later, when a woman with a mole on her face went to Lamotte for treatment, he pronounced it cancer and offered to cure it for $75. He was arrested for practicing medicine without a license.

One of the 20th Century's most infamous cancer scams, the Hoxey Clinic, also operated for a while in Michigan. Hoxey's treatment, which featured arsenic as its active ingredient, had been discovered by a "Dr." John C. Hoxey, a dabbler in veterinary medicine and faith healing who unfortunately died himself of cancer in 1919.

Despite that bad publicity, four years later, his son, Harry M. Hoxey, launched the Chicago-based National Cancer Research Institute and Clinic. Following a string of widely reported patients' deaths linked to the Hoxey treatment and a series of lawsuits, Hoxey bounced around to several midwestern towns until in 1930 he sought the metropolitan market in Detroit.

By hiring a renegade M.D. to evade Michigan's medical practice law, Hoxey lasted two years in the Motor City, before shifting to Wheeling, West Virginia, Atlantic City and other urban centers. Hoxey was careful not to ship his medicines across state lines and, despite decades of litigation by the FDA, he managed to stay in business until 1960.

Modern medical science has made vast strides since the days when tomatoes were considered a cause of cancer. Many forms of cancer can now be arrested if caught in time. Still the disease remains modern mankind's most-feared enemy. And until a positive cure is discovered, undoubtedly there will continue to be charlatans who profit from cancer and other such loathsome diseases.

Preachers on Horseback

Methodist minister Seth Reed, a giant of a man who the Indians named "Straight up in the sky".

Crazy Allen" leaped from the makeshift pulpit, eyes blazing. The congregation parted like the Red Sea as he made for the drunken rowdies at the rear of the room. Seizing one in each hand, the Reverend Allen pitched them into the muddy street. Shaking his fist at the crowd of "devil's loafers" watching from the tavern across the street, Allen spun around, strode calmly back to the pulpit, and returned to exhorting his now very attentive brethren.

The Reverend James B. Allen's mission, to put the fear of the Lord in Michigan frontiersmen, allowed little room for personal trepidation. His pulpit antics and loud, animated preaching, to say nothing of his bellicose response to hecklers, had won him the title of "Crazy Allen." No sir, it would take more than "a couple of the devil's two-legged whiskey tubs" to dampen his evangelical zeal.

It was 1859, and the itinerant Methodist minister had battled the devil across southern Michigan, preaching at the top of his lungs at camp meetings, churches, schoolhouses, or wherever he could gather an audience.

"Michigan," Crazy Allen had confided to his diary, "was the worst backslidden state in the union." Now he would launch a campaign for the Lord in Oxford, a small village in northeastern Oakland County, which was noted especially, Allen had heard, for "rum, profanity, and irreligion."

Oxford soon learned that Crazy Allen was en route to bolster the efforts of the local pastor. Certain local tipplers, who liked their town the way it was, planned a hearty reception for this evangelistic troublemaker. The two drunks Allen had booted from his meeting constituted only the opening salvo. The following evening a gang of bullies bashed a battering ram against the wall of the church, but Allen outshouted even that intended interruption.

At the next service, a crowd of vigilantes ambushed Allen as he walked to the church. As they surrounded him the ringleader read by the light of flickering torches a notice that if Allen "did not clear the town within 24 hours, the penalty would be a coat of tar and feathers, well put on."

Without a reply to his accosters, Allen walked calmly to his pulpit and informed the congregation of what had transpired. Then Crazy Allen dug into his pocket, flung some coins on a table, and addressing the gang that skulked in the rear of the church, he thundered: "Here is the money with which to buy the tar and feathers, and you may select a rail to suit yourselves. But be assured of this one thing: if you do not cease your ungodly deeds and let me and the meeting alone, the Lord will kill every devil of you!!" From that point on, Methodist church meetings operated much more smoothly in Oxford.

Untutored, fearless, resourceful, and dedicated, Crazy Allen was one of Michigan's more colorful roving preachers. He was a soldier in a Bible-armed missionary army that fanned out across the peninsulas during pioneer days. Like those who first brought law and medicine, these traveling ministers trekked circuits across desolate frontier tracts.

They wallowed through marshes and swamps, swam horses across rivers, slept in the woods, and were serenaded by wolves. It took uncommon men who could place propagation of the gospel above their own survival. They were out to save souls, and in so doing brought a much -needed civilizing influence to lonely pioneer cabins.

Nineteenth century Protestant churches took seriously the mandate to proselytize, and the region of the old Northwest Territory beckoned as a fertile ground for missionary zeal. Presbyterians, Baptists, Congregationalists, and other denominations employed both roving ministers and missions to spread their particular dogmas.

The Methodists, however, seemed best equipped for success on the frontier. Their democratic organization appealed to frontiersmen, and preachers who eschewed book -learning for old-fashioned western stump oratory spoke their language. What's more, self-sacrificing itinerants carried out their mission with a zeal that almost guaranteed results. The Methodists movers and shakers became the most numerous clergymen in the midwest, and the Methodist Church ultimately gathered the largest flock.

Methodism had been introduced to Michigan in 1804. Five years later the Reverend William Case became the first preacher in charge of the Detroit circuit . By 1811, Elder Henry Ryan sometimes assisted Case in his Michigan endeavors. Ryan, a frontier character with more than the usual fervor, greeted fellow itinerants from the saddle with "Drive on, Brother, drive on! Drive the devil out of the country. Drive him into the lake and drown him!"

Case and Ryan would ride into a frontier settlement, stable their horses, and walk arm-in-arm down the street singing a hymn. When they had attracted a crowd at the market place, they mounted some makeshift rostrum such as a butcher's block and began exhorting. Sometimes hecklers would try to trip them off their platform or set fire to their long, flowing hair, but the missionaries paid little attention to the devil's interruptions.

Methodist preachers gained a reputation for fiery speech that spared no class of listeners. The Reverend Joseph Mitchell preached in the Council House at Detroit in 1816 to Governor Lewis Cass and all the local civil and military men of note. Pointing his finger and glaring at the high-ranking congregation, he shouted, "You Governor! You lawyers! You judges! You doctors! You must be converted and born again, or God will damn you as soon as the beggar on the dung hill." The next day, Cass sent Mitchell five dollars and a note proclaiming it was the best sermon he had ever heard.

Yet the Methodists made little genuine progress in Michigan until the 1820s. When the completion of the Erie Canal in 1825 offered easier access to Michigan territory, a flood of settlers arrived in Detroit and began moving west. Pioneers spread across the southern part of the state, pre

Camp meetings such as this offered salvation and entertainment to frontier society.

-empting land, building log cabins, and establishing towns. Increased population brought a greater commitment in the number of Methodist preachers.

By the 1830s Methodist circuit riders ranged across Michigan's frontier. The church hierarchy included ordained bishops, presiding elders, preachers in charge, and deacons as well as non-ordained preachers and exhorters. Few were stationed in one locale. As founder John Wesley had said, "Should I preach to one congregation steadily for two consecutive years, I would preach myself as well as the people, dead as stones." Even bishops considered it their duty to travel and preach.

In 1830, ten circuit riders served the entire populated section of the state. The Reverend Elijah Pilcher was assigned the Ann Arbor circuit that extended from Dearborn to Jackson and included all the setttlements in between. He was expected to preach 26 places every four weeks. In 1831, Pilcher earned a revised circuit that emcompassed Washtenaw, Jackson, Calhoun, Branch, Hillsdale, and Lenawee counties. It took him 400 miles of travel every four weeks to complete the circuit of 27 stations.

The first settlements lay along the Territorial Road roughly equivalent to the present I-94 and the Military Road which is now U.S. 12. At the western end of his circuit, Pilcher blazed the first north-south road with a hatchet. He routinely slept in the woods, spurred his horse across swollen streams, and waded ice-covered swamps on nearly frozen feet. The young preacher remembered seeing plenty of deer and other game and longed for a gun, but his scruples prohibited carrying a firearm on the Sabbath.

Life on the circuit demanded as much equestrian skill as it did religious fervor. Circuit riders jogged along on large, strong horses astride good saddles. Their roomy saddlebags contained all their earthly possessions including clothing, blankets, food, and books. Spills and water-soaked saddlebags were major catastrophes.

Presiding Elder James Gilruth arrived in 1832 to take charge of the entire southern Michigan district. He kept a detailed diary that records many vexing experiences with his mount. In January of 1834, when leading his horse, it pranced, kicked him in the leg, and dragged him through the snow. In May, his steed suddenly slipped and pitched the elder over the animal's head into the mud. Bruised and dirty, Gilruth struggled throughout that day to free the horse, which had become mired up to its belly.

Things were little better two years later. In June of 1836, high water at a stream near Plymouth forced Gilruth to strip naked, wade across with his saddlebags held high, and then lead his horse across. At the next stream, when he tried to gauge the water's depth with a long stick, the stick broke and he pitched in head first. He recorded, "I was now in a sad pickle."

In addition to full-time itinerants who traveled incessantly, a number of ministers homesteaded on weekdays and set out each weekend to preach. The Reverend William Daubney pioneered on Gull Prairie in the 1830s. Each Saturday afternoon he would stuff Bible and hymn books into his saddle bags and ride to some schoolhouse, tavern, or private home in Kalamazoo, Allegan, or Barry county for church services the next morning. In addition to all-night rides of 20 to 50 miles, he journeyed an additional 15 miles or so on Sunday to hold prayer meetings elsewhere. Monday mornings found him hard at work back on his farm.

Far-flung circuits, miserable roads, and bitterly cold weather caused a number of ministers to regard appointment to Michigan as a form of punishment. When James T. Robe learned that he was to have the Kalamazoo circuit in 1832, he believed that his superiors were trying to get him to resign. His territory included all the area north of the St. Joseph River, and from Climax west to Lake

Michigan.

Robe became the first minister to ride into the tiny settlement named Bronson, after its founder. He preached the first sermon in what would become Kalamazoo in Titus Bronson's log cabin on Arcadia Creek. During the next five years, Robe also pioneered the gospel in Allegan, Climax, Comstock, Galesburg, and Schoolcraft. After surviving several decades on various Michigan circuits, Robe was retired with a pension. He returned to Kalamazoo where he died in 1888.

As more and more pioneers flooded into Michigan during the mid-1830s, and Kalamazoo, site of the Federal Land Office, boomed, Methodist circuit riders became a common feature in frontier society. Easily recognizable by their plain, dark apparel, old-fashioned straight breasted coat, high collar, wide-brimmed fur hat, flowing hair, and well-stuffed saddlebags, traveling preachers made an impression on many a pioneer as they plodded along wilderness trials.

Circuit riders were meticulous about making their appointed rounds, even if it meant traveling all night. A pioneer audience was not easily assembled and, if disappointed, would likely be missing the second time.

Elder William W. Crane, who covered the Jackson circuit in the 1840s, was once so racked with fever that he could not get on or off his horse unaided. He rode into a lumberyard in Leslie and crawled off onto a tall pile of boards. Despite illness, his horror of disappointing a congregation pushed him to complete his rounds. Such determination gave rise to the frontier adage: "It's so cold there's nothing out but crows and Methodist preachers."

Pioneer congregations, who gathered at no small sacrifice themselves, expected a rousing sermon for their trouble. Circuit riders knew their exhortations would have to keep sinners on the straight and narrow path until they returned in a month or longer, so they usually gave heroic performances. As opposed to their colleagues in more

The Reverend James T. Robe thought his superiors were trying to get him to resign when they assigned him to the Kalamazoo Circuit in 1832.

refined denominations who had studied theology in college and wrote out complicated sermons, Methodist preachers were self-taught graduates of "Brush College." The reading of sermons was frowned on by Methodist doctrine; instead, itinerants "took a text and exhorted" for several hours on end.

But while ministers who met the same congregation every Sunday needed to prepare a different sermon each week, itinerants could use the same well rehearsed pulpit oratory on their varying audiences. Untold hours in the saddle ruminating over yet more diabolical ways whereby sinners might spend eternity, yielded firery masterpieces that had a telling effect on pioneers isolated in the deep woods.

Circuit riders combined a rough-and-tumble delivery suited to frontier tastes with a mighty voice to earn the title "shouting Methodists." A Congregationalist minister in Charlotte in the 1840s thought his Methodist counterparts acted as though "the Lord were deaf or they lived so far away from Him that they could only with difficulty make Him hear." The Reverend Manasseh Hickey of Battle Creek preached so loudly at an Indian camp meeting near Saginaw the audience named him "Big Thunder." When the Reverend Abel Warren of Macomb County encountered a bear in his path late at night, he threw himself forward in the saddle and uttered a yell "such as only a full-fledged Methodist preacher could furnish voice to give," and the beast crashed into the underbrush. Crazy Allen said, "If the Lord don't want me to shout, he mustn't tickle me with salvation."

Given the poor acoustics of pioneer meeting houses, loud preaching served as more than an expression of exuberance. The Reverend Gilruth attracted crowds that packed cabins and overflowed into the yard. He would stand in the doorway or near a window and preach loud enough for all to hear.

Once when he was preaching from a doorway near Plymouth, a pack of dogs became excited by the loud noise.

They ran back and forth into the cabin barking. The preacher gave one a kick that sent one animal head over heels out the door without missing a word of his discourse. Shouting Methodists routinely dealt with other inconveniences, including a deaf old man who sat in the pulpit with his ear trumpet cocked to catch every word, as described by Caroline Kirkland in her autobiographical account of Michigan in the 1830s.

Henry H. Riley, whose *Puddleford and its People* ,published in 1854, offers a humorous look at everyday life "in pioneer Constantine", described a typical Methodist log-chapel sermon. The Reverend Bigelow Van Slyck spent two hours "following up the manifold sins of his congregation," and naming particular individuals. All the while, he was competing with barking dogs racing up and down the aisle, screaming infants, and an old lady taking snuff:

"Bigelow closed in a most tempestuous manner. He was eloquent, sarcastic, and comical by turns. He had taken off nearly all his clothes, except his pantaloons, shirt, and suspenders; a custom among a certain class of western preachers. Streams of perspiration were running down his face and neck; his hair was in confusion; and altogether, he presented the appearance of a man who had passed through some convulsion of nature, and barely escaped with his life."

Most preachers, however frenzied they might become, were fastidious about their apparel. A long single-breasted coat with a straight collar buttoned tight was the usual pulpit uniform. While a coat could be saved for duty during the sermon, trousers were a different matter. Many itinerants owned only one pair. "Big Thunder" Hickey wore a hole in the knee of his pants while shingling the roof of an Indian mission. When he had to preach the next day, he tied a bandage around his leg to conceal the hole and pretended to limp.

The Reverend Stephen Woodward, who organized a new

Elder William W. Crane prematurely wore himself out
while traveling the Jackson Circuit in the 1840s

circuit around Grand Rapids in 1845, patched his clothes until they fell to pieces. When his pants wore through at the knees, he cut them off and sewed them on backwards. Once while on his way to Okemos to preach, he ripped open his only pair of pants while mounting his horse. Because he had no undergarments on, he knew he was "in a sad plight." Fortunately he was able to borrow a pair to complete his circuit.

Such embarrassing sartorial emergencies stemmed from the ludicrously low salaries paid circuit riders. Bachelor preachers officially earned $100 a year and married men twice that amount. Out of that allotment, the man of God was supposed to feed both himself and his horse, clothe himself, and buy whatever books he needed.

Collecting the full salary from the local conference often proved another trial. In 1841 Stephen Woodward, for example, received only $37 in cash during his first year on the Livingston circuit. During his first seven years of service, he received less than $500 in total. By 1848 Woodward had married, but the official board at the Lyons circuit allowed him only $80 a year. In 1840 Sylvester Cochran, a Vermontville minister, wrote to complain that he had received only five dollars cash in two and a half years.

Itinerants supplemented their meager salaries by boarding around the circuit whenever possible. These free accommodations were typical of a frontier society and no better nor worse than what the pioneers had for themselves. When the Hastings circuit was established in 1841, the Reverend Daniel Bush, for example, was fortunate to gain the use of an upper, unheated room in a log cabin for his parsonage. When private homes were unavailable, ministers had to pay for their lodging at hotels. One tavern keeper near Monroe allowed preachers credit for sermons. A long sermon rated 25 cents and a short one 50 cents.

The Reverend Seth Reed, who served in the Grand Rapids

area in the 1840s, was once knocked off his horse by a tree limb. His frightened horse ran to the next cabin where Reed usually made a stop. The homesteader caught the horse, stabled it, and told his wife to get a chicken ready because the preacher was on his way.

Chicken dinners were a special treat on the frontier and usually reserved for an honored visitor such as a preacher. The Reverend Elnathan Gavitt thought the chickens recognized the danger and, as he approached a farm house, would "make for the barn or coop and stand there with tears in their eyes until I departed."

Normally a preacher got whatever sleeping accommodations were available, sometimes sharing a bed with other family members. But when a bishop or pre-siding elder paid a visit, families gave the best they had.

The Boutwell family, located near Ann Arbor, were honored to put up Presiding Elder Henry Colclazer one night .They fixed him a special bed at the head of a ladder in the log loft and even hung sheets up for his privacy. Colclazer, who wore a wig, hung it on the bedpost for safe keeping overnight. When Boutwell arose early in the morning and spotted the wig, the first he had every seen, he began yelling that the Indians had scalped the minister. When Colclazer jumped out of bed at the alarm and Boutwell saw his bald head, he ran out screaming " Murder! Murder!" Poor Boutwell never did fully live that one down.

Humorous incidents periodically enlivened life on the circuits, but normally Methodist preachers were a serious lot. They saw frontier society as being in a sorry state. Sinners teetering on the brink of damnation seemed little cause for hilarity. In fact, many seemingly innocent recreations, including dancing, were considered sinful. The Reverend Riley C. Crawford of the Shiawassee circuit was mortified while preaching at the funeral of a child when he picked up the family Bible and a number of playing cards fell to the table. Methodists who wore gold watches, jewelry, ruffles, or even flowers were flirting with the devil. When a fancily-dressed young woman glanced into Crazy Allen's tent at a camp meeting, he leaped up, twanged her dangling earrings, and recited:

"Diddle, diddle, diddle,
Your're as proud as the devil"

Prominent among spiritual problems on the frontier were ardent spirits. The Reverend William Page credited Grand Rapids with having 200 barrels of whiskey but only one of flour in 1836. Distilleries were one of the first pioneer enterprises in numerous communities, and it was a rare barn-raising that did not feature all the raw liquor that could be drunk. Intemperance was one of the few available recreations.

Ministers themselves somtimes fell prey to vice. Elder William Crane railed against the speculative horse -trading practiced by many itinerants. To use their superior shrewdness in judging horseflesh was but another form of gambling, he argued. Other preachers succumbed to the oldest form iniquity - the temptations of Eve.

Presiding elders held a pretty tight rein on the younger preachers while undergoing their apprenticeships. It was expected that circuit riders remain single for the first four years of service, and when contemplating marriage they were required to consult with their brethren before the proposal. Some, like Elnathan Gavitt, were generous enough to turn over likely partners to fellow itinerants nearing the end of their probationary period.

Yet, despite all precautions, incidents flared. A minister was publicly rebuked at the 1838 annual conference for marrying a lady "not of religious character." Worse yet, a preacher in Grand Rapids was expelled for adultery in 1836. Three years later a Tecumseh parson was convicted of trying to seduce the wife of one of his colleagues.

FIRST M.E. CHURCH IN MICHIGAN.

INTERIOR OF SAME.

Built in 1818 on the River Rouge six miles west of Detroit, Michigan's first Methodist church was a 24 x 30 feet log cabin.

But cases of ministerial back-sliding were exceptions to the rule. Most circuit riders led lives that were models of piety, devotion, and zeal. Many prematurely wore themselves out through long sleepless nights in the saddle and exposure to the elements.

The Reverend Crane, for example, had spent 15 years on Michigan circuits by the time he was 45. While he was traveling with a younger colleague, a woman near Battle Creek fixed him a special bed because she thought him to be an old man.

By the Civil War, the pioneer era had largely vanished from southern Michigan. Communities erected churches and sought permanent ministers. More sophisicated audiences wanted seminary-inspired sermons. Minsters were allowed to marry earlier in their careers and congregations competed for the best candidates with offers of more lucrative salaries.

Circuit riders fast became a thing of the past in all but the more isolated districts of the state . But succceeding generations would long remember the heroic sacrifices, noble devotion, and colorful character of the preachers on horseback.

Call Girls, Con Men and Crazy Ladies

Lydia Smith, who wrote about being treated most
foully at the Kalamazoo State Hospital.

Thousands of volumes crowded the two dimly-lit rooms of the shop located in a run-down Detroit neighborhood. Books packed two rows deep covered every inch of wall space. Stacked cardboard boxes of books littered the floor, and here and there a great tumbling heap of tomes reared up like a literary volcano. The only order I could detect was that those closest to the door had been acquired most recently. The perfume of old leather bindings and the faint vanilla-like smell of browning paper mingled with a stronger scent. I knew most certainly that untrained cats lived here. That and the nagging memory of the egg yolk I had seen lodged in the proprietor's bushy beard perhaps explained why I was not having much luck. I had spent nearly an hour scanning the shelves, poking into boxes, and carefully excavating mine shafts into the monolithic mounds of volumes.

The book-club editions of second-rate novels, the innumerable broken sets of outdated encyclopedias, and 19th-century theological publications had failed to stir my interest. I was nearly ready to give up, skunked I thought to myself,sniffing again the cat scent. Then I saw it.

An old pebbled-cloth spine peeked out from near the bottom of a leaning tower of books. Down on my hands and knees, I made out the faded gilt lettering, *Life in an Insane Asylum*. My heart leaped. I knew it was a rare book about the Kalamazoo State Hospital. I had heard about the edition but had never seen a copy. An arm load at a time, I worked my way down the stack and the treasure soon lay in my hands.

The binding was in good condition, the contents seemed complete, and yes ,indeed, it was Lydia Smith's account of the alleged horrors she had suffered in Kalamazoo. But the prize was not yet mine. Since none of the books in the shop were priced, I still had to deal with the proprietor.

Now book collecting is a sport, a game with certain rules. Finding desirable books is fun, paying for them less fun, and getting them home and gloating over them a lot of fun. Any unsporting philistine can acquire practically any rare book that exists by commissioning someone to find it and arming that someone with a blank check. Rarity, physical condition, desirability, and other factors determine the monetary value of a used book. Value can also be enhanced by association factors, that is, when someone of significance inscribed or owned the copy. First editions are usually more valuable than later printings. But there are more worthless first editions than otherwise. As Charles Lamb said, "First editions are not nearly so rare as tenth editions," and rightfully so.

The value of a particular book to a sporting collector is determined by an equation - desirability over price equals a sale. If the book is sufficiently rare, however, there is always the question of whether you will ever encounter another copy. Sometimes if you want the book badly enough, you have to bite the bullet. I was prepared to pay a fair amount for *Life in an Insane Asylum*, but not a crazy price.

If the shopkeeper set too high a figure, the book would remain with him and the cats, and all my excitement of discovery would be in vain. A little strategy seemed in order. Based on the general run of his stock, I judged the proprietor to have a less-than-thorough knowledge of the used-book trade.

But I had had enough experiences with this sort of an establishment to know that some proprietors try to use their customer's knowledge against them. That is, if I wanted something out of all this junk, it had to be valuable and would be priced accordingly. Strategy, definitely, was in order.

I picked out half a dozen worthless volumes, nestled the prize within the pile and set them on the counter. "How much for the books?" I asked, trying not to stare at the egg in his beard. As I held my breath, a pair of grimy hands pawed through the books, roughly flipped open covers, and fanned the pages of each volume in turn. People hide money in books, you know.

"These are very old books, first editions," he whispered, "I want three dollars apiece."

"Fine," I said. "I'll take this one." I grabbed my find, quickly laid three dollar bills on the counter, and made for the exit. "You can have those others for two dollars apiece," he croaked. "No thanks," I said, and Lydia and I waltzed out the door.

The thrill of owning an artifact from the past - a beautiful example of the art of book-making, a first edition that may have been handled by the author, or a valuable item that others covet - inspires many book collectors to hunt for their trophies. I admit to all of these motives but also justify my pleasures of the chase by using the volumes I acquire. I seek little-known books that offer details about Michigan's past. Information on traditional aspects of history is readily available. I want to document the colorful, the unusual, the entertaining incidents that never made the textbooks.

Besides, it's relatively easy to write about generals, prosperous entrepreneurs, politicians, and other pillars of the community, but what about the lunatics, hookers, and rogues? Who will tell their stories? Their lives, no matter how sordid, should not be swept under the rug but studied to see what progress, if any, our modern society has made in dealing with social problems. Their narratives, incidentally, also make fascinating reading.

I carefully examined my copy of *Life in an Insane Asylum*. Lydia Smith had had her behind-the-scenes look at the Kalamazoo State Hospital privately published by a Chicago firm in 1879. I noticed something that I missed during the excitement in the bookstore. Faintly stamped on the spine was "Vol. I."

An announcement for the next volume pasted on the back

endpaper promised additional sensational information taken from the diary of an attendant. Bibliographies revealed, however, that Volume II of the expose' mysteriously never appeared. Lydia Smith's likeness gazed benevolently from the frontispiece, a pleasant, middle-aged woman of erect carriage and firm resolve. I found no trace of insanity in her visage, but after reading some of her poetry appended to the narrative, I wondered.

Lydia, according to her narrative, had been treated most foully during the nearly six years she was incarcerated in the huge brick structure on what was then called Asylum Avenue but was sagely renamed Oakland Drive by later real estate promoters. Chloroformed and bound by her husband, the 31-year-old native of Jonesville arrived at the hospital in August of 1866.

Her troubles began that first night when a matron knocked out five teeth with a wooden wedge as she forced medicine down her throat. Things got progressively worse - severe beatings, painful constraints, and attempted murder by Superintendent Edwin Van Deusen. Lydia finally escaped in 1872, thanks to a friendly attendant who had been fired, and made her way back home to friends in Jonesville.

The book read like a dime novel, interesting but hardly believable. Van Deusen, I knew, had been a highly respected physician and a public-minded citizen who had donated the money for Kalamazoo's first public library in the 1890's.

Several months later, I secured a scarce volume that made me go back and take another look at *Life in an Insane Asylum*. It seems that Lydia Smith was not alone in her accusations.

A former inmate, a Mrs. Newcomer, had brought a lawsuit against Van Deusen on complaints similar to Lydia Smith's allegations. A number of other "grave reports that patients were oftentimes treated in a harsh, cruel, and barbarous manner" were also in circulation.

The Michigan legislature appointed a joint committee to

investigate the complaints. Committee members interviewed scores of witnesses, mostly former employees, and published a 864-page report containing transcripts of examinations and other evidence. The committee indeed found "that instances of carelessness, cruelty, and abuse on the part of the attendants toward patients have frequently occurred in the Asylum." Superintendent Van Deusen and his staff of physicians, however, were completely exonerated of charges of improper conduct. The committee also recommended a series of internal policy changes that would prevent such abuses in the future.

It took me another five years to round out the trilogy on 19th-century Kalamazoo's "cuckoo's nest." Daniel Putnam joined the staff of the State Hospital as chaplain in 1859, the year it opened. After his retirement, he published in Detroit in 1885 his memoirs. *Twenty Five Years with the Insane* offers a balancing view of what went on up on the hill. Its pages are filled with stories of interesting cases that came under his observation. A patient obviously suffering from delusions of grandeur posted the following order:

ORDER NO. 2
To E.H. Van Deusen, M.D., Principal
George C. Palmer, M.D., 1st. Assistant
E.g. Marshall, M.D., 2nd. Assistant
KALAMAZOO MICHIGAN
INSANE ASYLUM
My Dear Sirs, Bros.,Comps, and Sir Knights: You will instruct all in authority under you, from this time, henceforth and forever, to obey my royal will and pleasure in all things that I may desire or ask for; to open all doors at my command, furnish all necessary information, and attend in every respect to my royal will and pleasure. For my yoke is easy and the burden is light.
Amen! Amen! Amen!

Kalamazoo's lady electrical doctor, S.E. Morrill, suggested eye pain sufferers shock their optic organs back to health.

Royal Palace of the King of Kings and Lord of Lords, Kalamazoo, Mich.

(Signed)

King of Kings and Lord of Lords

Next to the section on life among the insane, I shelve Dr.S.E. Morrill's *Treatise of Practical Instructions in the Medical and Surgical Uses of Electricity*, published in Kalamazoo in 1882. An inscription on the fly leaf indicates that the book originally belonged to a nurse in Hall D, Michigan Asylum for the Insane. The author, one of Kalamazoo's first female physicians, preferred to be known as an electrician. She based her book on clinical experiences of 15 years. Doses of electricity, Dr. Morrill proposed, could cure medical problems ranging from cancer to snake bites. Cases of diarrhea, cholera, tumors, smallpox, headaches, lumbago, hemorrhoids, catarrh, and carbuncles needed but the healing effects of an electromagnetic field.

Dr. Morrill also found her 19th-century version of shock therapy excellent for hypochondria, hysteria, kleptomania, and insanity. Patients simply sat in a chair and immersed their feet in a basin of water. The good doctor cranked up the juice, applied one electrical wand to the upper spine, inserted the patented nickle-plated rectal electrode, and watched the fireworks. It is not known how many State Hospital patients Dr. Morrill produced with her quackery.

A more reputable Kalamazoo physician, Dr. Rush McNair, provided a glimpse into another little-documented aspect of life in Kalamazoo in his *Medical Memoirs of Fifty Years*, published in 1938. Amidst reminiscences of his first delivery and other early medical experiences, McNair paused to describe the city's "red-light district," where "half a dozen red lights showed the way to hell." These houses of ill repute were located on the other side of the tracks on Kalamazoo's north side.

According to McNair, Madame Net Warner's bordello catered to a more aristocratic clientele, but Big Mary's place was larger and more popular. Madame Net rode regally up town in a hack. Errands took her to various dress shops for lingerie and cosmetics and to the drug store for Lysol. A number of her rouged-up staff usually accompanied her, waiting in the hack and generally promoting business among curious bystanders.

Big Mary, on the other hand, a robust and muscular specimen who did her own bouncing, plodded to town in a more prolitarian fashion. Pedestrians got out of the way and shopkeepers gave her all the credit she wanted. Her word, McNair remembered, was as good as gold. Mary's teenaged niece, whom she was raising, sometimes accompanied Mary to town. Any hustler who made a pass at the young lady soon regretted it. When McNair treated the niece for typhoid fever, Mary confided, "I'm trying to bring that girl up a Christian, damned if I ain't."

Big Mary Shaffer and her house of ill repute periodically earned a little free publicity in the Kalamazoo newspapers. On May 31, 1886, one of Mary's employees, who had "been living the life of a sport for a year," took an overdose of morphine. On October 19, 1886, a federal judge in Grand Rapids fined Mary $100 for the sale of liquor. She "planked down a $100 bill." The Kalamazoo Gazette ran a feature on February 4, 1887, about a 16-year-old "doortender" at Mary's place. The girl's father had the police pick her up, but she thought the "county jail a worse place than Mary's."

Dr. McNair remembered that reformers had dimmed the red lights on the north side, and the scarlet ladies set up business elsewhere. The October 20, 1887, issue of the Gazette confirmed that Mary had "vacated her rendezvous on 'the dock' and her female companions are scattered throughout the city."

Further information on this particular aspect of

Kalamazoo's past eluded me. Then one lucky day a book-hunting adventure turned the trick, so to speak.

Returning from a trip to the Upper Peninsula last fall with my friend and antiquarian bookman from Niles, Ralph Casperson, we stopped to investigate a little antique shop in Manton. A bookcase in the rear of the room held 30 or 40 assorted volumes. I, being taller, scrutinized the higher shelves, and Ralph took the lower. It did not take us long to decide they held nothing but junk.

Then I noticed a slim green binding with no title on the spine. I always pull out a book without a title, and as a result have found some real treasures missed by others.

The title stamped in gold on the front cover read *A Magdalen's Life.* Too bad, a religious tract, I thought. Well, maybe it was printed somewhere in Michigan. The title page, however, carried no imprint, only *A Magdelen's Life* by Georgie Young, "Price $1.00." Flipping through the pages, I spotted references to several Michigan place names. I paid the $2.50 penciled on the volume, tucked it under my arm, and we were soon back on the road.

The drive from Manton to Reed City passed quickly as we took turns reading excerpts from the text. I had discovered the autobiography of a prostitute who had plied her trade in the late 19th century in Grand Rapids and Kalamazoo - a book so rare that the *National Union Catalog* locates only two copies in the entire country. Even the Library of Congress lacks the title.

Georgie Young was born in South Creek, Pennsylvania, in 1858. Her mother, a poor widow with six children, moved to Illinois three years later. When Georgie was 11, her oldest brother swindled his mother out of an inheritance which he invested in Michigan timber. In 1872 the family moved to Sand Lake in northern Kent County.

Things went well until Georgie accompanied an older brother to the State Fair in Grand Rapids that fall. She got lost and was befriended by a young hooker who introduced

Scarlet women enjoy their morning stogies.

her to a boyfriend. The Grand Rapids "sharper" married the 15-year-old girl under false pretenses, abused and starved her, and she soon found herself on the road to ruin. Actually it was the railroad, and Georgie wound up at Kalamazoo's Grand Rapids and Michigan Railroad Depot, which still stands at the corner of Michigan Avenue and Pitcher Street.

Naive Georgie and a street-wise painted lady caught a hack to a run-down, back-street dump known as "The Dock." They got lodging at what Georgie thought was a boarding house, but she wondered when the proprietor, Miss Alice, greeted them in "a long white wrapper and no sleeves." Her suspicions were confirmed later that night when Miss Alice called down the hall: "Come girls; gentlemen are in the parlor!" Georgie met the rest of the gang after breakfast the next day as the ladies of the evening cut cards to see who would buy their morning cigars.

Georgie tried running away from her red-light routine and caught a train for Elkhart. But after a series of misadventures with Irish Annie, Old Mother Thompson, a certain traveling man from Toledo, and a stint at the Detroit House of Corrections, she landed back in Kalamazoo. She bounced around to a number of local establishments, including "The Cottage" run by Miss Minnie. Georgie eventually worked her way up to become the madame of her own house in Grand Rapids, where she ended her narrative.

Not all the hustlers who worked Kalamazoo were women. J.P. Johnston, a notorious con man who operated throughout the midwest, described his checkered career in *Twenty Years of Hus'ling*. The volume, first published in 1887, became a best seller. In 1904 he authored an autobiographical sequel, *What Happened to Johnston*, and it contains a chapter about a Kalamazoo caper.

Johnston's particular racket at the time was the sale of gyp jewelry. He moved from town to town before customers noticed the green stains left by their gold rings. Several

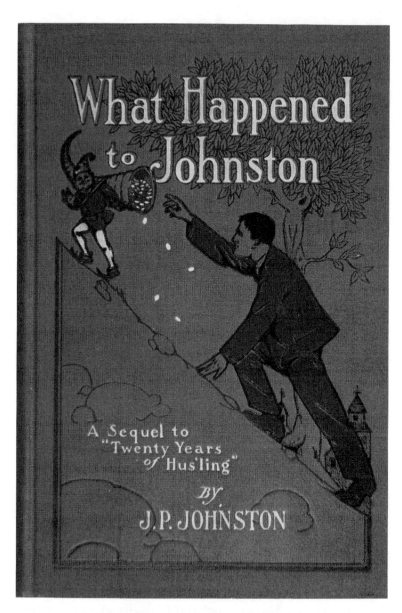

The cover of "Gyp" Johnston's 1904 book
in which he described a Kalamazoo caper.

Michigan cities had passed local ordinances requiring an expensive daily license for transient merchants to prevent fly-by-night operations. Johnston, therefore, secured a letter from a Chicago showcase manufacturer regarding an order for store fixtures that could not be completed in less than two months.

Following a stay in Jackson, Johnston moved into Kalamazoo. He rented a vacant store on South Burdick Street, set up a huge room full of bogus stock and began advertising in every paper in the country. Next he hired 26 employees, mostly young women, at one dollar per day. Six clerked in the store.

Johnston instructed the others to keep on their wraps and to leave the store, walk around a couple blocks, re-enter the store, look around at the merchandise, and repeat the performance all day. Johnston's employees created the appearance of a bustling business that drew in other shoppers. Within three days, his large store was packed every day from 3 to 11 p.m., and all 26 clerks were "kept busy wrapping up goods and taking in the cash."

When the police chief stopped in to inquire about the required license, Johnston handed him the letter about the furniture as proof of his intention to remain in business and walked away. For six weeks, during the pre-holiday shopping season, Johnston's jewelry outlet did an immense business. At 11 p.m. on Christmas Eve, three horse-drawn drays arrived at the rear of the store and within an hour, Johnston's staff had his remaining stock packed up and waiting at the railroad depot. Next stop, Indiana.

While in Kalamazoo, Johnston had reported the theft of a gold watch. A few days after he skipped town, he received a nice letter from the police chief stating that they had the thief in custody, but unless Johnston returned to prosecute they would have to release him. Johnston wrote that he "thought it would be better for the thief to get out of jail than for me to get in, and I'd just remain where I was."

J. P. Johnston was not the first nor the last con artist to fleece the Michigan public. "Yellow Kid" Weil, self-styled "master swindler" and author of a colorful autobiography published in 1948, arrived in Parchment during the bleak days of the Depression in 1933. His mission was to sting Jacob Kindleberger, president and founder of the Kalamazoo Vegetable Parchment Company.

I have told the story of how he succeeded in *Kalamazoo: The Place Behind the Products*, based on Kindleberger's manuscript account of the scheme. To make a long story short, Wiel convinced Kindleberger over a period of months that he was a wealthy entrepreneur interested in buying the paper company. When he gained Uncle Jake's confidence, he switched his interest to a bogus stock transaction and netted thousands on the deal. But Weil's autobiography provided details Kindleberger could not have known.

Weil credits the Parchment scam with being the first use of Chinese stooges. Kindleberger had shown little interest in the scheme until Weil brought in some Chinese investors who had reputedly discovered a new process that would revolutionize papermaking. Since the Chinese had originally invented paper, the idea seemed plausible to Kindleberger. Actually the orientals were three employees of a Chicago laundry whom Weil had decked out in fancy ceremonial clothing and hired at ten dollars a day.

Weil and the Chinese investors made several appearances in Parchment, carefully inspecting the plant. On the final trip, however, Weil nearly got stung himself. About 50 miles outside of Chicago, the Chinaman who was driving suddenly pulled the car over. Weil and his partner had a bag containing thousands of dollars in cash in the back seat with them, money to impress Kindleberger. They both figured the orientals intended to rob or kill them. Weil related what happened next:

"Why are you stopping?" I asked.

"For a showdown," answered the spokesman for the

"Yellow Kid" Weil in all his unrepentant glory.

three Chinese.

"Whats wrong?"

"You're making a lot of money on this deal?"

"We expect to," I admitted.

"But you only pay us ten dollars a day."

"Thats correct," I said. "What do you want?" I was sure now that he wanted a big cut.

"Ten dollars is not enough," he replied. "We get twenty dollars a day or we don't go another foot." I felt like laughing, but I gravely agreed to raise their pay. They smiled, the driver started the car, and we went on. They placidly went through the paces, and we had no more trouble with them. Mr. Stimson (Kindleberger) came through for us with $15,000 on the stock deal."

Yellow Kid Weil, J.P. Johnston, Lydia Smith, and Georgia Young penned intimate glimpses into the darker side of life in Kalamazoo. It is tempting to wax nostalgic over the good old days, but their rare documentation tempers the many sugar-coated sources.

Michigan's past contains many other colorful episodes. Wherever there are accumulations of old books, you can look for me, digging among the forgotten sources that constantly prove truth is stranger than fiction.

SOURCES

CHAPTER I.
Altman, Peter. "History of Aviation in the State of Michigan." *Michigan History Magizine*. Vol. XXII (Spring 1938).
Barnum, Phineas T. *Struggles and Triumphs or Forty Years' Recollections.* Buffalo, 1879.
Cuming, John. "Up, Up and Away: The Story of Ballooning in Michigan." *Chronicle.* Vol. 13, No. 3 (Fall, 1977).
Harper's Weekly. 7 August 1875.
New York Times. 17 July 1875 - 26 August 1875.
Wilson, James Grant and Fiske, John, eds. *Appleton's Eyclopedia of American Biography.* New York, 1888. 6 vols.

CHAPTER II
Cramp, Arthur J., ed. *Nostrums and Quackery.* Chicago, 1911, 1921, 1936. 3 vols.
Holbrook, Stewart H. *The Golden Age of Quackery.* New York, 1959.
Massie, Larry B. and Schmitt, Peter J. *Kalamazoo: The Place Behind the Products.* [Woodland Hills. Cal., 1981].
Walton, Esther. Interview. Hastings, MI. December 1986.
Young, James Harvey. *The Toadstool Millionaires.* Princeton, N.J., 1961.

CHAPTER III
Charlevoix, Pierre, *Journal of a Voyage to North America...* London, 1761. 2 vols.
Foster, Lillian. *Wayside Glimpses, North and South.* New York, 1860.
Hoffman, Charles F. *A Winter in the Far West.* London, 1835 2 vols.
Keating, William H. *Narrative of an Expedition to the Source of the St. Peter's River...* Philadelphia, 1824.
Latrobe, Charles J. *The Rambler in North America.* London, 1835. 2 vols.

Martineau, Harriet. *Society in America.* Paris, 1837. 2 vols.

Mason, Philip. *A Legacy to My Children...* Cincinnati, 1868.

Porteous, Archibald. *A Scamper Through Some Cities of America...* Glasgow, 1890.

Ruxton, George F. *Adventures in Mexico and the Rocky Mountains.* New York, 1848.

Scott, James L. *A Journal of a Missionary Tour...* Providence, R.I., 1843.

Shirreff, Patrick. *A Tour Through North America...* Edinburgh, 1835.

Swan, Lansing. *Journal of a Trip to Michigan in 1841.* Rochester, N.Y., 1904.

CHAPTER IV

Brannon, W.T. *"Yellow Kid" Weil.* Chicago, [1948].

Butler, William R. *Behind Prison Walls: The Story of a Wasted Life.* Chicago, 1916.

Davies, William H. *The Autobiography of a Super-Tramp.* New York, 1917.

Doty, Sile. *The Life of...* Detroit, 1948.

Johnston, J.P. *Twenty Years of Hustling.* Chicago, 1888.

Sharpe, May Churchill. *Chicago, May, Her Story.* New York, [1928].

CHAPTER V

Alphadelphia Society Papers. Bentley Library. University of Michigan.

[Durant, Samuel W.]. *History of Kalamazoo County Michigan.* Philadelphia, 1880.

Golab, Eugene O. *The "Isms," a History and Evaluation.* New York, [1954].

Mayer, Elizabeth M. *Yes, There Were Germans in Kalamazoo...* Kalamazoo, 1979.

Noyes, John Humphrey. *History of American Socialisms.* Philadelphia, 1870.

Primitive Expounder. Alphadelphia, Michigan. Vol. II, No.

15 (12 June 1845).

Thomas, N. Gordon. "The Alphadelphian Experiment." *Michigan History.* Vol. LV., No. 3 (1971).

Van Buren, Anson de Puy. "The Alphadelphia Association." *Michigan Pioneer Collections.* Vol. V (1882).

CHAPTER VI

Bonner, Richard E., ed. *Memoirs of Lenawee County, Michigan.* Madison, Wisc., 1909. 2 vols.

Horan, James D. *The Pinkertons.* New York, 1967.

Horan, James D. and Swiggett, Howard. *The Pinkerton Story.* New York, 1951.

Pinkerton, Allan. *The Model Town and the Detectives.* New York, 1876.

CHAPTER VII

Blair, Walter, ed. The Sweet Singer of Michigan. Chicago, 1928.

Cyclopedia of Temperance and Prohibition. New York, 1891.

Daniels, W.H. *The Temperance Reform and Its Great Reformers.* Cincinnati, 1878.

[Day, William F.]. *Leaves From the Pineries. No. 1.* 4 page tract. Detroit, N.D.

Heimann, Robert K. *Tobacco and Americans.* N.Y., [1960]. Kellogg, John Harvey. *Dyspepsia, Its Causes, Prevention and Cure.* Battle Creek, 1879.

_____. *The Household Monitor of Health.* Battle Creek, 1891.

_____. *Plain Facts for Old and Young.* Battle Creek, 1886.

_____. *Sunbeams of Health and Temperance.* Battle Creek, 1888.

_____. *Tobaccoism or How Tobacco Kills.* Battle Creek, 1922.

Livermore, A.S. *Brief Sketch of the Life and Work of...* Saginaw, 1890.

Lockwood, Guy H. *How to Live 100 Years.* Kalamazoo,

[1912].
Morrill, S.E. *A Treatise of Practical Instructions in the Medical and Surgical Uses of Electricity.* Kalamazoo, 1882.
Parish, Julia R. *The Poems and Written Addresses of Mary T. Lathrop.* N.P., [1895].
Post, Charles W. *The Modern Practice, Natural Suggestion, or, Scientia Vitae.* Battle Creek, [1894].
Putnam, Daniel. *Twenty-five Years With the Insane.* Detroit, 1885.
Record of Service of Michigan Volunteers in the Civil War - Seventh Michigan Cavalry. [Kalamazoo, 1903].
Sabin, Ransom. *The Home Treasure.* Battle Creek, 1890.
[Smiley, Joseph B.]. *The Meditations of Samwell Wilkins.* Kalamazoo, 1886.
CHAPTER VIII
Greely, Adolphus. *Three Years of Arctic Service.* New York, 1886. 2 vols.
Israel, Edward. Correspondence. Local History Room, Kalamazoo Public Library.
Kalamazoo Gazette. 1884.
Lanman, Charles. *Farthest North.* New York, 1885.
Todd, A.L. *Abandoned.* New York, \[1961].
_____. "Edward Israel: Michigan's Artic Pioneer." *Michigan Alumnus.* Spring, 1961.
CHAPTER IX
Barrett, J.O. *The Spiritual Pilgrim: A Biography of James M. Peebles.* Boston, 1871.
Bingay, Malcolm S. *Of Me I Sing.* Indianapolis, 1949.
Cadwallader, M.E. *Hydesville in History.* Chicago, 1922.
Carson, Gerald. *Cornflake Crusade.* N.Y., [1957].
Catalogue, Dr. Peebles' Pamphlets and Books. N.P., N.D.
[Chase, Warren]. *The Life-Line of the Lone One...* Boston, 1858.
Drs. Pebbles and Burroughs: Specialists. Battle Creek, [1900].
Flowers, B.O. *Progressive Men, Women and Movements of*

the Past Twenty-five Years. Boston, [1914].

Gardner, Washington. *History of Calhoun County, Michigan.* Chicago, 1913. 2 vols.

Hardings, Emma. *Modern American Spiritualism.* New york, 1870.

History of Calhoun County, Michigan. Philadelphia, 1877.

Lowe, Berenice Bryant. *Tales of Battle Creek.* Battle Creek, 1976.

Massie, Larry B. and Schmitt, Peter J. *Battle Creek: The Place Behind the Products.* Woodland Hills, Cal., 1984.

Cramp: *Nostrums and Quackery.*

Peebles, James M. *Seers of the Ages...* Chicago, 1903.

Pond, Mariam Buchner. *Time is Kind: The Story of the Fox Family.* New York, 1947.

Underhill, A. Leah. *The Missing Link in Modern Spiritualism.* New York, 1885.

Van Buren, Anson De Puy. "History of the Churches of Battle Creek." *Michigan Pioneer Collections.* Vol. 5 (1884).

Whiting, R. Augusta. *A Biography of A.B. Whiting.* Boston, 1872.

CHAPTER X

Cutler, H.G., ed. *History of St. Joseph County,* Michigan. Chicago, N.D.

Dunbar, Willis. *Michigan, A History of the Wolverine State.* Grand Rapids, [1965].

Dury, Wayne L. *White Pigeon, Prairie, Township, Village, Chief.* [Manchester, Tenn., 1989].

History of Allegan and Barry Counties, Michigan. Philadelphia, 1880.

History of St. Joseph County, Michigan. Philadelphia, 1877.

Hoffman: *Winter in West.*

Latrobe: *Rambler in North America.*

Martineau: *Society in America.*

Shirreff: *Tour Through North America.*

Silliman, Sue L. *St. Joseph in Homespun.* Three Rivers, 1931.

"White Pigeon's Grave." *Michigan Pioneer Collections.* Vol. 10, (1886).

CHAPTER XI

Dunbar, Willis. *Kalamazoo and How It Grew and Grew.* Kalamazoo, 1969.

Hagar, Dave. "Women Led this 1912 Labor Battle in Kalamazoo." *Kalamazoo Gazette.* 19 September 1982.

Kalamazoo Gazette. 6 April 1855.

Massie and Schmitt:

Kalamazoo. Michigan Bureau of Labor and Industrial Statistics. Annual Reports. Lansing, 1884-1920. Title varies.

Perry, Mrs. George A. "Women's Employment." *Twenty-Sixth Annual Report of the Secretary of the State Board of Agriculture of the State of Michigan...* Lansing, 1887.

Report of the Michigan State Comission of Inquiry into Wages and the Conditions of Labor for Women... Lansing, 1915.

CHAPTER XII

Allegan Gazette. 4 September 1933 - 22 September 1933.

Boone, Ilsley. "Nudism On Trial At Allegan." *The Nudist.* December, 1933. *Chicago Herald and Examiner.* 22 Sept. 1933.

Gay, Jan. *On Going Naked.* Mays Landing, N.J., [1932].

Hoffman, Clare E. Scrapbooks. Allegan Public Library.

Kalamazoo Gazette. 7 Sept. 1933 - 21 Sept. 1933.

Lester, Hugh C. *Godiva Rides Again: A History of the Nudist Movement.* New York, [1968].

Merrill, Frances and Mason. *Nudism Comes to America.* New York, 1932.

Nudism Exposed As Told by an Ex-Nudist. N.Y., [1934].

Pahl, John. Interviews. Allegan. 1986.

People vs Fred Ring, et. al. Allegan County Circuit Court

File. 1933.

Strange, Julian. *Adventures in Nakedness.* New York, 1934.

Traver, Robert. *The Jealous Mistress.* Boston, 1967.

CHAPTER XIII

Chase, Alvin W. *Dr. Chase's Third, Last and Complete Receipt Book and Household Physician.* Detroit, 1887.

Cramp: Nostrums and Quackery.

Holbrook: *Golden Age of Quackery.*

Hitchcock, Homer O. "On the Supposed Causal Relationship Between Cancerous Diseases and the Use of Tomatoes as Food." *Sixth Annual Report of the Secretary of the State Board of Health of the State of Michigan.* Lansing, 1878.

McNair, Rush. *Medical Memoirs of 50 Years in Kalamazoo.* [Kalamazoo}, 1938.

Young: *Toadstool Millionaires.*

CHAPTER XIV

Buley, R.Carlyle. *The Old Northwest: Pioneer Period.* Bloomington, Ind., 1950. 2 vols.

Caster, Elisha E. *A Memoir of James B. Allen.* Detroit, 1866.

Cole, Maurice F. *Voices From the Wilderness.* [Ann Arbor, 1961].

Hawkswell,John,compiler. *Autobiography and Miscellaneous Writings of Elder W.W. Crane.* Syracuse,N.Y., 1891.

Kirkland, Carolyn. *A New Home, Who'll Follow.* New York, 1839.

Lockwood, Charlotte. *Church on Main Street. A History of First Mehodist Church, Jackson, Michigan.* Jackson, 1947.

MacMillan, Margaret B. *The Methodist Church in Michigan: The Nineteenth Century.* Grand Rapids, [1967].

Pilcher, Elijah H. *Protestantism in Michigan...* Detroit, [1878].

Reed, Seth. *The Story of My Life.* Cincinnati, 1914.

Riley, Henry H. *The Puddleford Papers.* New York, 1856.

Simpson, Mathew, ed .*Cyclopedia of Methodism*. Philadelph
-ia,1882

CHAPTER XV

Brannon: *Yellow Kid.*

Johnston: *Twenty Years.*

Johnston, J.P. *What Happened to Johnston.* Chicago, 1904.

Massie and Schmitt - *Kalamazoo.*

McNair: *Medical Memoirs.*

Morrill: *Treatise of Practical Instructions.*

Putnam, Daniel. *Twenty-Five Years with the Insane.*
Detroit, 1885.

*Report of the Joint Committee of the Michigan Legislature
of 1879 on Alleged Mismanagement... in the Michigan
Asylum for the Insane at Kalamazoo...* Lansing, 1879.

Smith, Lydia A. *Behind the Scenes; or Life in an Insane
Asylum.* Chicago, [1878].

Young, Georgie. *A Magdalen's Life.* N.P., N.D.

INDEX

A

Adams, John Quincy, 110
Adams, Samuel Hopkins, 28, 30
Adrian, 15, 60 92, 93,97, 99, 100, 102, 103, 113
Albion, 29, 37, 146, 147
Alcock, Douglas, 190, 195
Alexander the Great, 186
Algonac, 24
Allegan 56, 165, 185-199, 222
Allegan County, 164, 185-190, 221
Allegan County Fair, 193
Allegan Gazette, 195
Allegan News, 190
Allegan State Forest, 186, 199
Allen, James B., 216, 217, 224, 229
Alma College, 110
Alphadelphia Society, 56, 78, 82-90
Alphadelphian Tocsin, 86, 87
American Card Co., 176
American Medical Association, 27, 28, 40, 210
Angier, Mary, 189-199
Ann Arbor, 82, 125, 189, 203, 220, 228
Appomattox, 109
Arcadia Creek, 164, 222
Atlantic City, 214
Atlantic Ocean, 17
Auburn, New York, 112
Australian Red, 67-70

B

Bacon, Francis, 78

Badgley, F.C., 33, 34
Baker, Albert M., 93, 96, 97, 99, 100, 106
Bannister, W.D., 15
Barnum, P.T., 19, 140
Barret, J.O., 150
Barry County, 221
Barthel, Kurt, 187
Battle Creek, 29, 39, 114, 117, 119, 138-141, 143, 146 -148, 150, 151, 162, 198, 224
Battle Creek Sanitarium, 39, 116
Beaver County, Pa., 78
Bellevue, 82, 83
Benton Harbor, 59
Berlin, 187
Berrien County, 170, 172
Bidwell, Austin, 73
Bidwell, George, 73
Bingay, Malcolm, 153
Bixby, Alonzo F., 103, 104
Black, John, 99, 104
Black Hawk, 158
Bloomer, Amelia, 148
Blowena, 28
Bogart, Humphrey, 120
Boone,Ilsley, 195, 196
Boston, 80, 150
Boston Commons, 110
Boston Company, 164
Bourbon, Ind., 30
Bow, Clara, 120
Boyd, R.W., 113
Brainard, David, 123, 128, 135
Branch County, 220
Brant, J.W., 37

Hoffman, Clare E., 192, 193, 195, 198
Holland, 95, 195
Houghton, 64, 65
Hoxey, Harry, 214
Hoxey, John C., 214
Hussey, Erastus, 140
Hyde, William H., 154
Hyde Park, Il., 22
Hydesville, N.Y., 141

I

Ihling Bros. Everard, 181
Illinois, 48, 50, 157, 210
Illinois Envelope Co., 182, 187, 189
Illinois River, 42
India, 45
Indian Removal Act, 46
Indiana, 56, 79, 88, 165, 210
International Ladies Garment Workers Union, 175
International Nudist Conference, 195
Ionia, 17
Irish Annie, 242
Israel, Edward, 122-137
Israel, Joseph, 125
Israel, Mannes Magnus, 125
Israel, Tillie, 124, 125

J

Jackson, 29, 33-36, 56, 65, 82, 220, 244
Jackson, Andrew, 46
Jackson Circuit, 222
Jackson County, 82, 220
Jackson Prison, 59, 62, 104, 106

James, Jesse, 106
Jefferson, Thomas, 193
Johnson, Jack, 29
Johnston, J.P., 59, 62-67, 242, 245
Jonesville, 52, 235
Junction, the, 56

K

Kalamazoo, 29, 33, 39, 40, 50-54, 56, 57, 113, 117, 119, 124-127, 135, 137, 162, 164, 167-182, 185, 187, 189, 193, 201, 222, 235, 240, 242, 244
Kalamazoo Corset Co., 170, 172, 175, 176, 181
Kalamazoo County, 48-50, 82, 86, 90, 160, 221
Kalamazoo Gazette, 56, 167, 169, 192, 193, 239
Kalamazoo Ladies Library, 179
Kalamazoo Loose Leaf Binder Co., 179
Kalamazoo Medicine Co., 40
Kalamazoo Pant & Overall Co., 170, 173, 181
Kalamazoo Paper Co., 181
Kalamazoo Playing Card Co., 182
Kalamazoo River, 78, 83, 86, 139, 162
Kalamazoo State Hospital, 232, 234
Kalamazoo Twentieth Century Club, 179
Kalamazoo Vegetable Parchment Co., 245
Kane County, IL., 92
Kansas, 46, 157

Michigan Bureau of Labor, 169, 170, 173
Michigan Central Railroad, 49, 54, 95, 135, 139
Michigan Expositor, 93
Michigan Legislature, 60
Michigan Southern & Northern Indiana Railroad, 92-106, 167
Michigan State Board of Health, 30, 201
Michigan State Commission of Inquiry Into the Status of Working Women, 178, 179
Michigan State Fair, 65, 240
Michigan State Medical Society, 201
Michigan State Penitentiary, 33
Michigan Statesman and St. Joseph Chronicle, 165
Michigan Supreme Court, 103, 196, 198
Michigan Women's Christian Temperance Union, 113
Michillimackinac, 42
Miller, Fred, 185, 190, 192, 193, 195, 196, 198
Miller, William, 140
Millerites, 80, 140, 148
Mississippi River, 42, 45, 46
Mitchell, Joseph, 218
Mixer, Charles, W., 206, 207, 209, 210, 212
Mixer, S.S., 206-212.
Molly Maguires, 106
Monroe, 150, 227
Montgolfier, Joseph, 15
Montgolfier, Jacques, 15
Moore, Joseph H., 93, 100, 102

Moore, Julia, 114
Moran, Frank, 29
More, Sir Thomas, 78
Morey, Peter, 102-104
Morgan, F.P., 207
Morgan, John, 144
Morrill, S.E., 119, 238
Mountain Home Cemetery, 54, 137
Murray, Edward J., 193
Muskegon, 73

N

Napier, Charles, 95, 96, 106
Nashville, Il., 211
National Corset Co., 175, 176
Newark, 154
New England, 60, 139
Newgate Prison, 73
New Hampshire, 39
New Jersey, 147, 151
New York, 79, 82, 139, 140, 144, 147, 158, 187, 193, 198
New York City, 54, 73, 110, 175, 182, 195, 201
New York Graphic, 17
New York Times, 24
Nichols and Shepard Plow Works, 139
Niles, 29,30, 42, 43, 45, 48, 52, 53
Niles Democrat, 147
Norfolk, VA., 17
North Pole, 125
North Western Cancer Institute, 204
Northwest Territory, 46, 157, 217
Nottawa Sepee Prairie, 48, 49

Reed, Seth, 227
Republican Party, 209,
Reynolds, Henry A., 113
Riley, Henry H., 225
Ring, Fred, 185, 187, 189, 190, 192, 195, 196, 197, 198
Ring, Ophelia, 185, 187, 189, 190, 192, 195, 198
Rio de Janerio, Brazil, 73
Ripon, W.I., 90
River Oaks Park, 90
River Raisin, 157
Robe, James T., 221, 222
Rochester Democrat and Chronicle, 154
Rochester, IN., 212
Rochester, N.Y., 14, 52, 141
Rockford, IL., 211
Roosevelt, Franklin, 186
Roosevelt Hospital, 201
Rosenbaum & Sons Co., 182
Ruxton, George A., 54
Ryan, Henry, 218
Ryno, E.H., 37

S

Sabin, Ransom, 119
Saginaw, 108, 224
Saginaw Valley, 108
St. Albans, VT., 59
St. Clair River, 24
St. Clair, 203
St. Johns, Newfoundland, 128
St. Joseph, 70
St. Joseph County, 48, 157
St. Joseph-Kankakee Portage, 42
St. Joseph River, 42,221
St. Luke's Hospital, 29,30

Sand Lake, 240
Sanitary Laundry, 182
Savery, Asahel, 160
Sauk Trail, 158
Sawyer, Braxton Bragg, 198
Schoolcraft, 50, 162, 222
Schley, Winfield Scott, 135
Scott, James L. 53,54
Scotten, Daniel, 111
Seventh Day Adventist, 116, 120, 148
Seventh Michigan Cavalry, 108
Shaffer, Mary, 239
Shaker, 78, 87
Sheldon, Thomas, 160
Shetterly, Henry R. 82-84, 86, 88, 90
Shiller D.R., 210, 211
Shirreff, Patrick, 48, 165
Simon-Saint de Henri, 79
Sing Sing Prison, 59
Smiley, Joseph Bert, 113
Smith, Al, 198
Smith, Joseph, 80, 140
Smith, Lydia, 232, 235
South Bend, IN., 165
South Creek, PA. 240
South Haven, 22
South Seas, 109
Spanish American War, 135
S. Salomon & Co., 170, 181
Stanwood, J.H., 24
Stewart Hall, 148
Stuart, Augustus, 93
Stuart's Catarrh Tablets, 37
Stuart, F.A., 37
Sturgis, 52
Sturgis, Prairie, 53
Sullivan, John L., 110

Larry B. Massie is a Michigan product and proud of it. Born in Grand Rapids in 1947, he grew up in Allegan. Following a tour in Viet Nam as a U.S. Army paratrooper, he worked as a telephone lineman, construction laborer, bartender and in a pickle factory before earning three degrees in history from Western Michigan University.

He honed his research skills during an eight-year position with the W.M.U. Archives and Regional History Collection. He left in 1983 to launch a career as a freelance historian, specializing in the heritage of the state he loves. An avid book collector, he lives with his wife and workmate Priscilla, and their 30,000 volume library, in a one room schoolhouse nestled in the Allegan State Forest. Sons Adam, Wallie and Larry Jr., as well as a border collie named Maggie, and Jiggs, a huge saffron-colored feline, insure there is never a dull moment.

Larry and Priscilla Massie donned period costumes for their Celebrate the Great Lakes Chautauqua performances in 1989. (Photo courtesy Kalamazoo Gazette - Robert Maxwell, photographer)